The Pilgrim's Freedom

A retelling of the John Bunyan classic
The Pilgrim's Progress

ISBN-13: 978-0-9913445-2-9
ISBN-10: 0991344529

.

Please visit www.dharold.com

Blue House/Magoo
Publishing

For Tanya, who supported me

It Is My Hope

There is something coming.

A new way of looking at things.

A way that is surprising to some, unsettling to others, and an enormous relief to millions.

And it's been under our noses the whole time.

I'm not an optimist by nature. I'm what you'd call a spectator in life, an observer.

And life is not always pretty.

But I'm excited.

I'm excited about where things are going. I'm excited about what's presented in this book.

And I hope it generates conversation for many years to come.

D. Harold

February, 2015

Introduction

So why retell a classic?

Well, it depends.

If the classic is good, then great.

But if it's not good—

Ok, I'm just going to say it outright: *The Pilgrim's Progress* is horrible.

It reflects a view of God that is unattractive and deplorable. Instead of being 'good news,' it's patently bad news.

Progress' interpretation of what the Bible is trying to communicate turns the Christian endeavor into a bizarre caricature of itself. The main character is never settled in his soul. He never finds the peace and rest he's so badly trying to attain.

It's heart-wrenching.

On top of that, he's continually put through a battery of obstacles and tests in life seemingly sanctioned by none other than God himself—just to see if he's worthy and faithful.

And if that weren't bad enough....wait for it....*Progress*' view of theology *continues* to be the mainstream Protestant/Evangelical view.

Ouch.

That is why I wrote this book.

That is why it's so important.

And not only is a major revamp of *Progress*' theology needed, there's a larger arc to consider here as well: Is Christianity itself even an accurate reflection of what the Bible wants to communicate?

I believe what is needed is a rethinking of *everything* when it comes to Christianity and what is deemed to be the Biblical worldview.

There *is* a better way to view things.

And with this story, I hope to not only pave the way for a better Biblical worldview, but even more so, to lay a foundation that can carry humankind into a better future.

That is my hope.

So without further ado, come with me as we take a look at *The Pilgrim's Progress* from a more accurate, more positive, more useful, and more *Biblical* point of view.

Enjoy.

Chapter 1

The Pilgrim On His Treadmill

I walked around the world surveying all I could see.

I marveled at the good things, was disgusted by the horrible things.

All the evil nearly broke me.

Such contrast!

The ugliness! The beauty! Side by side!

So many conflicting thoughts and emotions stirred within me...I neared exhaustion trying to make sense of it all, so I found a nearby cave and went in. I lay down and fell asleep. I dreamt I saw a man in tattered clothes, walking on a treadmill with a Book in his hands.

He was forever walking, yet never arriving.

I felt sorry for him.

That's when I noticed a balance beam—yes, the kind used in gymnastics—stretched out in front of the treadmill. I saw him open the Book in his hands and begin to read, and when he did, he would begin to run faster on the treadmill.

In eventual exhaustion, he slowed down. Then he began to walk faster, to a quick trot. Then, as further exhaustion set in, he simply walked again.

Then he began to weep.

No longer able to control his inner emotions, he trembled as he walked and cried out, "What shall I do?"

The man, the treadmill and the balance beam stood in a vast, empty field. His house was nearby, within sight. Despite his condition, the man did not get off the treadmill. He did not go into his house to rest.

His wife and children came out of the house and called to him: "Come in! Eat with us, and rest!"

Drying his tears, the man seemed to double his resolve and responded to them, "Oh my dear wife and children, I am undone by this awful burden that lies heavily on my back. It's a burden we all must bear, and we will all suffer unto it for our lifetimes unless we find a way to be delivered."

But his wife and children just looked at him in confusion, for they were bright, happy and relaxed.

"What burden, dear?" his wife called out.

His children looked on at the wild spectacle, fearing their father was losing his mind.

The man did not answer them, but set his face forward on the treadmill, as if to steel his resolve.

His wife called out, "It's getting dark, honey, won't you come in?"

Getting no response, she went over to forcibly bring him in the house. But he shook her off. "No! This is something I must do. It's required of me by the Book."

She went away dejected, and she and the children went into the house.

Alone.

* * *

When morning came, they looked out the window at the man, still on the treadmill—walking slow, then gathering himself to a trot, then walking slowly again—all in repeated cycles, and never

2

stopping.

The Book was still in his hands.

His wife came out of the house, stretched her arms and smiled as the children ran gleefully past her to frolic in the fields. But they stopped and looked downcast as the woman called to her husband in love, "How do you feel, honey?"

"Worse and worse," the man reported.

He slumped his shoulders but did not stop walking.

His family began to get impatient and rude. "Then stop walking! Get off that crazy thing and come and eat...and rest!"

But he wouldn't stop walking.

So they took offense at his ridiculous resolve and tried to coerce him into the house by any means necessary—by insults, scolding, and even completely ignoring him for a time.

But none of it worked. He seemed locked in a comfortable contentment in his misery.

His family pitied him and prayed for him.

And the man continued to read his Book, and prayed as often as he could as required by the Book.

* * *

One day, deep in meditation as he walked on the treadmill, the man finally erupted: "What shall I do to be saved?"

He looked to one side and the other, as if he would suddenly hop off the treadmill and run into his house. Yet he stayed, for he felt it would be wrong of him to get off the treadmill; that dreadful things would happen if he did.

Then I saw a man approach the treadmill on foot. The approaching man said, "Hello. My name is

Freedom. Can I ask what you're doing and why you're so distraught?"

"Sir, I understand from this Book that I'm supposed to do exactly what I'm doing...for the rest of my life. I have to focus on my walk and never take my eyes off the balance beam. Not to the left or to the right. For straight ahead is where God is, and all else is the World, which is of the devil, and evil, and doomed to destruction."

"Huh," replied Freedom. "Well, I suppose you're in quite a jam then."

"Quite," the man replied caustically, sweating profusely. "But it's good. It's good to be here. This is where I want to be. I just have to love my enemies all the time and always forgive everyone every time they wrong me (God won't forgive me otherwise—Matthew 18:34-35). On top of that, I have to always love everyone no matter who they are, how they treat me, if they rub me the wrong way, or even if we simply don't enjoy each other's company. We have to be together and get along. We *have* to. I have to always do for others as I would want done to myself, always, all the time. I *have* to *always* do more for others than they ask of me, twice as much, or *more*. There is always more and more and more to do and it's never enough...it's exhausting really. But if I don't keep moving forward, then I'll be moving backwards. And no one wants that. Especially not me. And certainly not the one who wrote this Book. So I must push, push, push and push ahead forward, in growth and memorization of this Book, and in doing everything I can for other people all the time, always, all the time. I always have to live outside my comfort zone or God will be displeased. If I'm not *outside* my comfort zone I'm not doing what God wants me to do."

4

The man paused to take a breath, then continued with great consternation, "But the worst thing about it...The worst thing of all! The thing I can't seem to get out of my head, is that when I was born I was told this life would be restful and abundant, abundant in joy and peace...but it doesn't...it just doesn't....it doesn't make any sense!"

The man collapsed in heavy, exhausted sobs.

But only for a split second.

Realizing the danger of his error, that he was slipping *backwards* on the treadmill (*God forbid!*), he immediately got back up and started walking.

Freedom looked puzzled. Rubbing his hand on his chin, he asked, "Who told you all this? Where did you hear such things?"

"At church, of course," the man blurted. "And in this Book."

"So this, this...what you're doing here...this is....your *walk* with God?"

"Yes," the man spat, his agitation rising. "Isn't it obvious?"

Then he looked at Freedom with great guilt, but did not stop walking. "Oh! Oh....I'm sorry. I'm super sorry. I shouldn't have yelled like that. I didn't mean it." He looked forward again. "Errrrrgh! I *need* to control my temper! I *can't* treat people like that....Sir, I'm really sorry. I failed. I failed again. I didn't mean to make you feel bad." He gestured at the treadmill and balance beam. "This is all me...this...where I'm at. This is *my* problem. My burden to bear. You don't have to try and help me if you don't want to. I can do this on my own. I just have to buck up and make sure I stay outside my comfort zone, and everything will be all right in the end." The man momentarily looked longingly at his house, then back toward the balance beam. "No!

No...I *know* where I'm going. I know where this is going. It's for my own personal good and the good of others, and one day I'll be as Christ, I'll be *Christlike*, I'll love everyone as Christ loves them. Perfectly. Eventually." He nodded his head in quick, jerky motions. "Yes...Yes, it's for my own good. It's for my own growth and learning process."

Freedom looked confused. "For your own good? Are you some kind of masochist? What you're doing doesn't seem 'good' at all."

"It's called 'sanctification.' Suffering is part of the process," the man answered, almost mechanically. "Well, it's *most* of the process, anyway, when it gets down to it. This is just the way things are supposed to be. God wants it this way. Eventually I'll be like Jesus. If I just keep focusing on the balance beam, and make sure not to meander to the right or left, and keep going as fast and as hard as I can straight ahead." The man then repeated to himself—or chanted—in a low whisper, "Daily devotional time, daily prayer time, serving others, doing ministry, daily time set aside to read the Book, daily time to meditate on the Book, daily time to memorize the Book...serving others...loving God...worshipping God...giving my life as a 'living sacrifice.'"

And with that, despite his incredible exhaustion, the man sped to a quick trot on the treadmill.

Freedom frowned. "Looks to me like this is doing nothing at all. That you're getting nowhere. That really you're just staying in the exact same place."

"Don't try and talk me out of it!" the man yelled. "This is good! This is where I should be. It's what God wants. The Book tells me so. This is what I learned in church. It's called 'sanctification.' I know it looks bad. But really, it's good. It has to be this way. It's for my own good. This is my burden to bear. This is my journey. It's a lifelong process. It's a walk with God...that's what we call it. A walk with God. It's for a lifetime. And it's good."

Freedom stood for a moment in silence, then looked sadly at the man. Freedom looked this way and that, all around him, and thought to himself: *If this was a 'walk with God'...?* He saw a man walking, yes, but he did not see God. God was nowhere to be found.

With a downcast look, Freedom turned to walk away.

"But..." the man said suddenly.

Freedom turned.

"But..." he said again, without looking at Freedom.

"But..." he said once more.

"Yes?"

"But...I've been thinking...I'm really tired of this. And like I said, it doesn't make any sense with some of the other things I've read in the Book. So if..."

He paused.

"If...." the man had a pained looked on his face as if in fear of blaspheming the Spirit of God himself.

"Yes?" Freedom encouraged him.

"If there is any way to look at this differently...any way at all for me to get rid of my burden, I.....I will listen."

The pitiful man turned and finally looked at Freedom, but still kept walking. "I promise to listen. Just...just...just please help me. Or this burden will sink me."

Freedom took a step back, surveyed the

situation and said, "Ok, step off that thing and go into your house. Eat, rest, and be with your family."

The man looked forward again. "I know. That's what I'd thought you'd say. That's what they say, too, my family. But it's not as simple as that."

"Oh?"

"Yes. I know this Book is good. I know my church has good intentions. Before I can get off this treadmill, I need to understand. Help me to understand. I have lots of questions, and know not where to turn."

"Ok," Freedom sighed, disappointed this wouldn't be as easy as he thought. But he genuinely cared for the man, and liked him, so he stayed— "Ok, let's do this thing."

Chapter 2

The Pilgrim Moves Toward Freedom

Freedom stepped forward and gave the man a violent shove off the treadmill.

He hit the ground—hard.

"Ow!"

"Sorry, but it had to be done."

The man lay sprawled where he landed, head spinning, legs reflexively twitching. He grabbed at his head and legs in desperation. "I can't make them stop!"

"It will get better in time," Freedom said flatly. "Just take a minute. Take all the time you need."

After awhile, when the man had somewhat recovered, Freedom pointed into the distance. "See that narrow gate over there with the light on it?"

"Yes, that's the narrow gate Jesus talked about isn't it? About how hard it is to get to heaven, and how most people are on the wide road to destruction, and only a few will be saved by entering the narrow gate and..."

"Stop, boy. You're speaking like a damn fool."

The man was taken aback. "I am?"

"Yes. You promised to listen, right? So listen. First, no, that is not the narrow gate Jesus talked about. The narrow gate Jesus referred to actually has to do with the Mosaic Law, something no one is to follow anymore (Romans 7:6). But we'll get to that soon enough. Second, that light doesn't represent how hard it is to get to God, or the fact that only a 'few' will supposedly be in heaven while most go on to destruction. That light," Freedom pointed again with emphasis, "represents how hard it is to get *away* from God."

"Really?" the man marveled in disbelief.

"Yes. Now look at the wide open expanse before you." He waved his arms in a wide gesture. "All that room out there. All that area. All that infinite space out there..."

The man took a moment to look around. There was nothing on the horizon, or anywhere else for that matter, besides his house, the treadmill, the balance beam, the two men, and the small, faint light way off in the distance on the narrow gate.

"Wow, that's a lot of room!" the man remarked.

"Yes, it is. Ok, get up. You should be able to stand by now."

The man stood on shaky legs. He gave each leg a shake once or twice, then seemed fine.

"Good," Freedom declared.

The man started to walk forward.

"Ah ah ah! Where are you going?" Freedom asked.

"Well, this is where you tell me to start walking, right? To go out and take in everything I see. Take advantage of all that great expanse out there. It needs to be mined, explored, cultivated, used...I can't wait to get started! There's lots of work to be done. See ya!"

Freedom smacked his own forehead. "Oh, dear," he muttered. *Again, this is going to be harder than I thought...*

He walked forward and pulled the man back to his original place. "Stand here, please."

"But you said you were going to help me…"

"I am," Freedom said in exasperation. "Listen to me!"

"Ok," the man replied sheepishly, sufficiently chastised.

"Before we go any farther, what is your name?"

"Chris. But my full name is…"

"I don't care what your full name is. If you feel the need to tell me, tell me later."

Chris shrugged his shoulders and took a step back.

Freedom took a scrap of paper from his pocket. "First, I want you to understand one thing."

He handed Chris the paper.

Chris read it aloud: "Matthew 11: 28, 'Come to me, and I will give you rest.' Yeah! This is what I heard when I was born. It's fantastic isn't it? I'll be sure to memorize this! Thanks for the help! Thanks, that was great," and he started to walk away again.

"Boy! Get back here! You're killing me!" Freedom reached out and pulled him back once again. "No! You are not to move! At least not until I say so. Is that clear?"

"Ok, sorry." Chris looked at the note again, read a few lines, closed his eyes, and muttered the line over and over.

"What are you doing?" Freedom asked in surprise.

"Memorizing it," Chris replied, and closed his eyes and kept muttering.

"Stop! Ugh!" Freedom slapped his forehead again. "All you need to do is *read* it and understand what it says. One time! One time, boy! Jesus wants to give you rest. Give you *rest.* Can you understand that?" Freedom took a deep breath and sighed. *Man, I need a break for a little while.* "Now, I'm going to

11

give you some simple instructions. Very simple. Do you think you can follow them and not wander off again? Can you do exactly as I say?"

Chris thought a minute.

"*Can* you?"

"Yes, yes, I can. I will. I mean, yes, sir, I'll do whatever you say."

"Ok, good. Now do this. Lay down on the ground, right here, and go to sleep. First you need to sleep. You need to rest. Jesus mostly meant this in the spiritual sense I'm sure, but it doesn't hurt to take it literally once in awhile. At any rate, it's a good object lesson for you because you badly need some literal, physical rest. So I want you to do just that. Literally rest. For a good long time. As long as you need. As long as it takes. And when you awaken, I'll be here and we can continue talking."

"Ok, if you say so."

"I say so."

Chris lay down and yawned a wide yawn, "Good night."

"Good night. Enjoy some rest."

Freedom turned to walk away.

"Hey, man," Chris said from the ground.

Freedom turned around.

"Just wanted to say thanks."

"No problem."

And Freedom walked away.

Chapter 3

The Pilgrim Meets Religious And Jesus-Follower

I saw in my dream that Chris had barely closed his eyes when several neighbors stopped by from afar off fields.

They were in the habit of dropping in now and then to see how he was progressing on the treadmill.

When they saw him resting instead of running, they mocked and jeered, speculating he was probably trying to be 'spiritual but not religious,' and that simply could not stand.

They called to him demanding he return to the treadmill. Several voices tried to be persuasive. Others were quite threatening. Among the neighbors were two men; one named 'Religious' and another named 'Jesus-follower.'

Everyone in the crowd talked and pointed at once, mostly in displeasure and condemnation of what they saw. The commotion, as you can imagine, quickly roused Chris from his slumber. He addressed the crowd groggily. "Neighbors, why are you here?"

Religious took it upon himself to be their spokesperson and replied, "We're here so that you'll come back to us by jumping back on your treadmill where you belong." (For each had their own treadmills back home, and only left them to come and check on Chris and to keep him in line. His personal well-being was really not of their concern.)

"Yeah, sorry, I can't get back on that thing," Chris replied. "I'm tired of living like that. It doesn't seem right. There's got to be a different way to go about things. My friend Freedom is helping me. He can help you, too. I'm sure he won't mind. He should be along any minute..."

"We have no interest in changing our minds or considering any other way," Religious announced. "We are happy on the treadmills and want to stay that way. You should want that, too. Why would we want to change?"

Chris looked at them. "Don't you think if there's the least possible chance to get a taste of the peace, joy, and abundant life the Book speaks of it'd be worth it to throw it all away and consider a different way? Stay with me please and hear what Freedom has to say. See if what he says makes sense."

"Are you saying you're *not* experiencing those things on the treadmill?"

"Are *you*?" Chris asked incredulously. "Who among you is experiencing any of those things on the treadmill?"

Religious steeled his resolve. "We're not looking for things to be nice and easy and make sense *now*, dear boy. No, that's not what this is about. This is about good things coming *later*, rewards and such, for those who diligently seek it. By doing this, we are storing up treasures in heaven where neither moths nor rust destroy. And God uses suffering to get us where he wants us to go. He makes us suffer and be uncomfortable in order that we may become fully reliant on him. So that we put nothing we want

14

before him. The goal is to want him, and him only. Forever and ever. Anything that we want more than God is an idol, and that displeases him greatly. You can read it all for yourself, right there, in the Book."

Chris scratched his head, for he remembered reading a lot about idols and God being displeased with people for this reason in the Old part of the Book, but not so much in the New.

"We know what you're thinking. But believe us, it's in there."

Chris wasn't so sure. He knew this was the way things had been taught for centuries, but it just didn't add up. However, their argument was just convincing enough that his resolve began to falter. *Maybe they're right...*he thought. *After all, how could people be inaccurate for centuries....surely someone smarter than I must have considered what Freedom has been getting at. Why hasn't anyone ever seen what he seems to know?*

Chris decided to open his mouth. "Freedom seems to think there's a different way, a better and more accurate way to view and understand what's written in the Book."

"Oh, hogwash!" the crowd complained. "There's no different way to view things. It's been the same for centuries! It's been right and good all this time. Will you just join us again on our treadmills, or not?"

"No, because I've already been pushed off by Freedom. I'm sure it will only happen again."

"Hogwash again!" they shouted. "Consider yourself warned. You need to know that the president of the treadmill club, Pastor Hard Work, is very displeased and he along with us are considering kicking you out of the club. We will then not associate with you in any way until you decide it best (repent!) to get back on your treadmill. And by

15

the way, while you're away, you're still expected to keep up payments on your club dues. Just saying."

"So you will not join Freedom and I? Are you really going back to your treadmills?"

"We are. We have already put our hands to the plow. We must continue on our journey. We need to keep making progress."

"Ok, suit yourselves."

"Come, then," Religious said, turning to the man next to him. "Jesus-follower, you're my best friend. Let's go back with the others and keep doing things so that God will not be displeased or turn his back on us. We have acceptance only if we stay on the treadmills. You know that. People who jump off are crazy fools. They will have no rewards in Heaven, their lives will be burned up and they will be as those who barely escape the flames. They consider themselves wise in their own eyes, their pride has puffed them up. They are making and worshipping idols by putting their comfort before God (among other things), and God wants no other Gods before him. We must worship God, and God alone, and we must love him with all our heart, soul and mind. We all know this. The Book clearly says so, in the Old part and the New. So we must keep pushing on. Moving forward on our journey. If we're not moving forward, then we're moving backward. And then God would be displeased with us."

"I'm not so sure...," Jesus-follower said, to the shock of Religious. "If what this good man says has any merit, I'd like to consider it. Seems he has some legitimate questions and sincerely wants to understand why life under our system doesn't seem very abundant, joyful, peaceful or restful. I think the boy might be on to something." Jesus-Follower nodded his head. "Yes, I'd like to hear what this

Freedom fellow has to say."

"What? Are more fools being created as we speak?" Religious chided. "Don't be silly. Come back with us to our treadmills. Who knows what this nut-job might get you in to! What if he's wrong? Do you really want to risk it? Be wise and stay the course."

"No," Chris piped-in. "Come with us, Religious. I'm sensing there could be much to be gained by choosing Freedom. I'm sure we will learn of wonderful things. I'm also pretty sure what Freedom speaks of are things contained in the Book, and the truth of it will be confirmed by the very author of the Book himself."

"Neighbor Religious," Jesus-Follower added, "I have made my decision. I am going to stay here with this fellow."

Religious was indignant. "We're leaving! I will not be a party to such deceived and muddle-headed thinking! God is very displeased with you both, and God will be very displeased with us if we stay here any longer!"

And all the neighbors, except for Jesus-Follower, turned and left.

Chapter 4

The Pilgrim and Jesus-Follower Wait

I saw in my dream that Chris and Jesus-Follower were left alone in the field.

"So, Chris," Jesus-Follower asked, "do you know how far we need to travel to get where we're going? Shouldn't we get moving at once?"

"Well, actually, Freedom told me to stay right here and rest. He said this is the first step, and he seemed pretty adamant about it. He said he'd be back soon to give me more instruction."

"But there is a light way off in the distance, and a little gate. Isn't that the narrow gate Jesus spoke of? I think we need to go there."

"I thought so, too. But Freedom had a different, seemingly better, way of explaining the narrow gate. He was pretty vague about it but seems to know. I'm sure he'll explain it when he gets back. Remember to ask him if I forget."

"But from what I understand, we need to go on a journey to get what God has for us. We'll figure it all out as we go. It'll only make sense if we're moving forward," Jesus-Follower said.

Chris answered, "From what I understand, the Lord, the King of this country, has recorded all this in the Book. The message is, as I understand it, if we want it he will give it to us freely."

Jesus-Follower was ecstatic. "I'm glad to hear

of this! I can't wait. Let's go! Let's get going!"

"I said he gives it *freely...*"

"Salvation, yes, but then there's sanctification! It's a lifelong process. Let's go! My treadmill awaits!"

"No, *all* is given freely. It says so in Galatians 3. We are reconciled to God freely, and then we live with God freely. Anything we need, he gives. He's given us practically everything already, though (Ephesians 1)."

"But we grow *toward* him. We work *for* him and serve him each day. It's called sanctif..."

"I know. Sanctification. But after talking to Freedom, I'm not so sure that's what I read in the King's Book. And from what I understand, He cannot lie...Besides, I can't go anywhere anyway, even if I wanted to..."

"Why not?"

"Because of the burden on my back. It's growing. I can hardly move now, much less get myself on the treadmill. Where's that blasted Freedom? Where is he?...Look Jesus-Follower, I know this will be very hard for you, but let us sit down and rest."

A trace of a smile crossed Jesus-Follower's face, then he sat with Chris on the ground as they reclined on their elbows.

"Aaaaah," Jesus-Follower sighed. "You might be right. This is quite nice, actually."

"Pretty much beats the treadmill, doesn't it?"

"Mmmm. Yes. But I reserve the right to be skeptical of all this."

"That's fine. So am I. I'm trying to figure it all out, too. What you say we do it together?"

"Ok. Deal."

So I saw in my dream that Chris and Jesus-Follower pulled up their elbows, lay down, and slept a very deep sleep in the soft, cool grass.

Chapter 5

The Pilgrim Meets Mr. Worldly-Wise

Next I saw in my dream that Chris' slumber was soon disturbed by a faint noise afar off that kept getting louder and louder.

A man was approaching, who to Chris' eye was smallish, but grew larger and larger until he filled Chris' entire field of vision.

Feeling slightly anxious as to the development, Chris looked over and saw Jesus-Follower fast asleep. He decided not to disturb him and try to handle the situation himself.

The approaching man introduced himself as Mr. Worldly-Wise. He lived in the city of Everything Outside the Christian Religion. Chris lived in Christian Subculture, a suburb of Everything Outside the Christian Religion.

Downtown Christian Subculture had very narrow streets and encouraged everyone to be very small. But there was *loads* of room in Everything Outside the Christian Religion.

So Mr. Worldly-Wise was a very, very large man.

He was so large, in fact, that his fat rolls held shelves piled high with music CD's, iPods full of songs and millions of books and DVDs.

He was really quite a sight.

Chris looked at him, disgusted. "I know why

you're so big. You're the wide path to destruction. You have a lot of music with you, and I have to admit, it's good. Most of it's *really* good. Really, really, really good, in fact. But we have our own stuff. We have very little music, it's true, and what we have is mostly crappy. But the songs are about God, so that makes it ok and we should listen to it. Same with books and movies. We have ours, separate from you, and it's a small collection and most of it's pretty crappy. You have a lot of it, and, as I said, most of it's incredibly good. But again, you're the wide path to destruction, so we must stay away. So please don't offer me anything. Thanks anyway, but I'll stick to myself and my crap."

"Oh, I wasn't going to offer you anything," the large man said. "I was just wondering why you're sitting there with that huge burden weighing you down. What's that all about? Seems even though I'm enormous and have all this stuff on me, I can move more freely than you."

"That's because you're the wide path to destruction," Chris repeated again. "We are from Christian Subculture. We're different. Intentionally different. We're burdened because we're trying to do something difficult. We're going for the narrow road, the narrow gate, the road less traveled. And furthermore, God helps those who help themselves— I read that in the Book. We are loaded down on our journey of walking on treadmills with the balance beam out front, yes, it's true. And it's a very narrow beam. A very narrow one indeed. We cannot go to the right or the left, or we fall off and God is displeased. He'd be very displeased if I didn't accomplish all he has for me to accomplish in this life. God's plan for me is very narrow and specific, and my life is driven by a purpose, God's purpose for me....of course, He didn't really tell me in the Book what my specific purpose *is*, but part of the stress and burden of the treadmill is to figure that out, and never go off to the right or left of God's specific intention for me. It's all part of the *walk*. Doesn't seem very loving of God to do that to me, but it's the right way for sure. I know it. So I think I'll just get back at it."

And he made a move toward the treadmill.

"Sonny, I'd check your Book if I were you. I believe 'God helps those who help themselves' isn't in there. In fact, that saying was made popular by Ben Franklin, who had no intention of exposing the contents of the Book."

"Don't try to trick me!" Chris shouted. "I know you're trying to trick me! But it won't work! I know what I'm doing."

Forgetting he meant to get back on the treadmill, Chris sat down. "I'm going to sit right here and rest and wait until Freedom comes back to tell me how I may be relieved of my burden."

The large man looked at him. "Do you have a family? Wife and children?"

"Yes, but don't stain them either. I won't stand for it." Chris shook a finger at him...then stopped and thought a moment. "In fact, no. No, I don't have a family, or a wife, or children. So go away. Please leave me alone."

"Will you listen to a bit of advice, if I should give it to you?"

"Er, ah," Chris debated for a moment in his head, then thought, *well, it couldn't hurt to just listen...*"Ok, what've you got to say?"

"Get rid of your burden. You'll never be happy until you do."

"Right! That's what I'm thinking, too! Now if

Freedom would just get back here..."

"May I ask—Who told you to get off the treadmill?"

"A great man. A man called Freedom."

"Curse him!" the huge man spat sarcastically. "I've never heard more stupid or glaringly misleading advice in all my life! Stay on the treadmill, sonny! It's best for all of us. After all, if you and the others leave your treadmills, some of what goes on in my town will simply shut down. There's so much that's simply a reaction to how strongly we disagree with what goes on in your town of Christian Subculture. It could be disastrous for us and the security we take in how much we make fun of you—why, it'd all go up in smoke if you freed yourselves! We'd have nothing to point fingers at."

The man's mood became grave, and sad. "A quarter of what I carry with me will be gone. That would be tragic indeed. Those poor folks who get a sense of security and solidarity from poking fun at you and your churches...If you let the churches collapse, then all my folks are left with is...is themselves, and that would be horrible...they'd be left with nothing to hold them together, since it was all rooted in one fact: that 'the other' (that's you all over here) existed, and it was stupid and harmful. No, no, no, my friend. You cannot be free. Please do not free yourselves. We cannot have that! Industries would be crippled! Lives would be shattered! It would be a full-scale tragedy, indeed!"

The formerly jolly man was truly sad. Then he gathered himself. "Listen to me now. Hear me because I'm older than you. You will be met with all manner of worries, painfulness, perils, sword, lions, dragons, and dungeons if you get yourselves to freedom. How could you have even begun to listen to a man like Freedom?"

Chris thought that most of the dangers the man named seemed extremely outdated, but let it pass. "Everything you mentioned is much better than living with this burden on my back," Chris said, then added quietly, "even though half the things you said are weird and have no relevance in this century."

"Well, how did you get that infernal burden to begin with?" the man blurted.

"By reading the Book, of course...Well, not so much from *me* having read it, as much as me reading it and being taught what it means by others in my town. We all go to the same church-club, you know."

"Yes, yes. But anyway, just as I suspected...the Book," the man scowled. "And now this Freedom fellow is telling you that very same book actually tells you the way to freedom, and *always has*?"

"Well, that's what I gather. It's just that he started telling me some stuff and then he went away. But he was supposed to come back and..."

"Ah, yes. And you fell for it. You fell for listening to things that are far above your understanding. Things far above your pay-grade, sonny. You are weak. You have compromised your manliness. He's made you want to venture into things he knows nothing about."

"You're wrong," Chris said with agitation. "I'm not weak. And I'm very manly. What I want is rest. I want some peace of mind and rest in my soul. That's what I'm looking for. What I'm looking for is to be relieved of my burden. Nothing wrong with that."

"But seek for it this way?" The big man thought for a moment. "Hey, how about this? How about I tell you a way where you can have a certain amount of freedom *and* still stay on your treadmill with your balance-beam thingy... and all the other stuff that seems so strange and unnatural to us in our town that we constantly make fun of....er...um...hrrrump!" the man coughed loudly. "Er, yes. You can have your cake and eat it, too! Yes, if you get back on the treadmill, your friends will not bother you AND you can be relieved of your burden."

"How, sir? How?" Chris asked eagerly.

"Bring all your stuff and move to my town. There you can simply walk at a steady rate on the treadmill. This is synonymous with being a good person in my town. You don't need freedom. You just need to accept the world as it can be seen and touched only by the five senses, and live this life to the fullest—and try not to hurt anyone around you too badly—of course—but if you do every now and then, then whatever....But hey," he brightened, "it's the way most of us live in my town. Sometimes we're on the treadmill, sometimes off. But we balance things and try to live in moderation. It works pretty well. No one needs this, this *freedom* you speak of. It sounds way too...way too...uh, way too *complete*. Yes, that's it. And I'm afraid, my dear boy, what you're asking for simply doesn't exist."

Chris thought a moment.

"Yes," the big man continued, "you could actually move into town with us! Bring your treadmill, yes, and even your silly balance beam there, erp, haha," he stifled a laugh, "er, ahem!...Just don't be on it all the time, please. And don't speed up and slow down and all that funny business we think is so funny. You can blend in, ole' chap, I assure you. There are other like-minded people such as yourself to be found there. People who enjoy religion and are friends of the religious.

Why, there are actual religious folks there as well. You will see. The food is good, the cost of living comparable..."

Chris thought a minute. "Well, that sounds pretty good. It gets my friends off my back, and I don't have to do the treadmill as much, or as fast."

The large man nodded in encouragement.

"And I can....hey," Chris stopped abruptly. "Can I bring my Book, too, or do I have to leave it behind? I like my Book. I don't want to leave it."

"Sorry, you can't..." the man began. "Well, I'll tell you what. You can bring it, but you can't read it or try to understand it. No problem having it with you."

"Hmmmm," Chris thought. "Not sure if I like that idea."

The man frowned.

Chris gained confidence. "I think I'm going to hold out for complete freedom. From top to bottom. I think life would be most abundant with this Book. I'm going to hold out that this Book will give me the most complete way to freedom anyone could ask for."

"Is that your final answer?" the man half-sneered.

"That's my final answer," Chris assured him. "In fact, I hope to see you again once I no longer divide the world into Christian Subculture and Everything Outside the Christian Religion, aka 'the World System.' I just remembered that Freedom told me he'd give me a better understanding of narrow gates and wide roads and all that stuff in my Book. I don't think all that stuff exists as I once thought it did."

"What about *Satan*?" the man waved his hands up and down in a silly motion. "Isn't he with me in my town? Always looking for a way to POUNCE!" He made his hands crooked like claws and thrust them at Chris in a silly manner.

"No, I'm not for certain, but I think God defeated that. It's finished. Has no power. Non-factor. Next!"

"Ok," the man sighed, putting his hands down and turning to go. "Suit yourself. But I think you're in way over your head, kid. I really do. But it's your decision. And please...please promise me you'll consider the implications on my town if everyone over here opts for freedom. Please think very, very, carefully about that. Don't take away the small bit of security we hang onto as you being 'the other.' We enjoy it so much, and it'd be a shame if it all went away and all we had to look at was...each other."

The large man frowned a moment then ambled away, waving his "claws" and chuckling as he muttered 'grrrrr.'

Chapter 6

The Pilgrim and Jesus-Follower Make A Fascinating Discovery

When Mr. Worldly-Wise had left, Chris looked around hoping to find Freedom had come back. But he was nowhere to be found.

So Chris lay back down in the grass and slept for many hours.

When he awoke, he found Jesus-Follower reclining in the grass, contentedly looking into the clouds.

Choosing not to bother him with details of his encounter with Mr. Worldly-Wise (since he wasn't sure it hadn't just been a dream), Chris said, "Jesus-Follower, I'm glad you're here. Tell me about yourself. It bothers me that no one else wanted to stay with us. I mean, if Religious had felt half as miserable and crushed under my burden as I felt on the treadmill, he wouldn't have gone away but stayed here with us instead. I really can't understand it."

"Yes, the treadmill is quite a burden, but I believe it's a good thing—at least in the long run. As for me, my treadmill is to pay attention to nothing but the words of Jesus spoken in the Book, and especially to *do* them. That's the key! It's not enough to *know* them, we have to *do* them. As it says in the book of James, 'Be not merely hearers of the word, but doers.' Some editions of the Book have Jesus's words written in red-letters so they are easy to find, read and follow. They are the most important words in the whole Book. Even if there are other words that seem a bit contradictory, or maybe we emphasize some red-letters over others, and though some are meant to be literal and others figurative, and so on...but anywho, we know we should stay with the red-letters. They are the safest thing to stick with if and when there is any confusion within the Book. For centuries there has been debate among the Learned of the Book as to why the red-letters of Jesus seem to clash with what that guy named Saul, later Paul, wrote in the Book. No one really understands this seeming difference, so we just direct people to hone in on the words and teachings of Jesus, and just do that with all your heart, soul and mind." Jesus-Follower smiled. "It's a safe bet, if you ask me. After all, Jesus was God. Not Paul."

"So you're not concerned with the seeming contradiction, or illogic, between the red-letter words of Jesus and the words of Paul?"

Jesus-Follower scratched his neck. "No. Jesus was God, and it seems to me what God says is final. Paul was just a man."

Chris leaned on one elbow and opened the Book. "So Paul wrote in Romans 8:1 'There is therefore now no condemnation for those who are in Christ Jesus.'"

"Yes."

"And Jesus said in Matthew 18:34-35 'In anger his master handed him over to the jailers to be *tortured*, until he should pay back all he owed. This is how my heavenly Father will *treat each of you* unless you forgive your brother or sister from your heart.'"

"Yes."

"Well, don't you see? It doesn't match up at all. Why hasn't anyone ever noticed that?"

"Well, they have. It's just that we've decided if there's a contradiction, Jesus' words are more important. After all, the religion is called "CHRISTianity, not PAULianity. Pretty simple if you ask me."

"Hmmmm." Chris stared intently at the Book. "There must be a way to understand what's going on here. The author of the Book wouldn't have been so vague and illogical...."

"I think things are just fine hitting the red-letters as hard as we can," Jesus-Follower said with enthusiasm. "After all, the Book's been around for centuries and centuries. How could no one have come up with a better solution after all these centuries?"

Chris rubbed his chin again. "Well, it has to be one or the other. There cannot be 'no condemnation' *and* the threat of ending up in God's torture chamber hanging over our heads all the time."

"Well, Jesus talked of the torture chamber, so that's what I go with. Therefore, I strive in all my energy and effort to forgive everyone every time they do something wrong against me, all the time. Better safe than sorry. Makes sense to me. It's the safe bet."

"But again," Chris butted-in adamantly, "that makes no sense. That would mean nearly everything Paul wrote is...*wrong*."

"Yes, but it's ok. We're Jesus followers. Jesus was God, not Paul. So God wins out. The red-letter words of Jesus are most important. Clearly. Therefore, I must strive to love God with all my heart, soul and mind. I must love others as I love myself, all the time. That's what he said to do. I must go the extra mile for everyone all the time. I must strive to lay up treasure in heaven, enter through the narrow gate, take the log out of my eye before removing the speck from my friend's eye. I must strive to meet the needs of everyone *all the time*, especially someone different from me who needs my help, and especially if they're my enemy...I must keep on..." Jesus-Follower suddenly looked distraught. "Oh my God! I'm just sitting here! I must get back to my treadmill! Why did I leave it? That was so dumb...Religious was right! Why did I listen to you? Why did I let you trick me?" He got up to go. "I have to get back there...have to get back to my treadmill."

"But..." Chris reached up and pulled him back down by the arm. "Ok, let's just calm down a minute."

Jesus-Follower sat back down. He took a deep breath, knowing talking things out calmly would be WWJD. "Please don't hold me back. The treadmill is the right thing to do. I know it is. What's the problem?"

Chris gave him a sideways look. "Just calm down. Something's not right here. I understand what you're saying and why you've come to your conclusions. I get it. You have good intentions and I understand that. Still...something is...something's just not right."

They both lay back, looking up at the sky.

Jesus-Follower let a huge puff of breath loose into the sky.

Chris sighed as well. "Man, I wish Freedom would get back here and explain all this. I can't understand what's taking him so long," he said with increasing frustration. "Doesn't he know we're waiting for him? He told us to wait."

"Yeah, I guess we'll just have to wait."

Chris sat up abruptly. "Wait a minute!"

"What?"

"You rattled off a lot of things Jesus said to do. And you're right. They are the red-letter words of Jesus. But..."

"But what? Is there a But? How can there be a But? Jesus said it, Jesus was God, and that settles it...no Buts."

"But....so you're saying you strive to follow the red-letter words of Jesus, right?"

"Yes, YES, of course! Haven't you been listening? I really think I ought to get back to my treadmill..."

"Wait," Chris looked him up and down.

"What are you looking at?"

"Have you ever done anything wrong since becoming a Jesus-Follower, something you'd call a 'sin'?

"Of course. Nobody's perfect..."

"But you still have both arms on you, I see....both eyes are still there...why haven't you chopped off an arm? Or gouged out an eye? Have you ever kicked something in unjustified anger? Why do you still have both legs?"

"Huh? Are you going crazy?"

"No, I'm very much sane. The problem here is that you're killing yourself to strive to follow the red-letter words of Jesus, and yet didn't he say to cut off body parts if they cause you to sin?"

"Well, yeah, but that's not to be taken literally. Everyone knows that."

"And yet, to always love your enemies, to *always* go the extra mile, to *always* do unto others as you would have them do to you, etc, etc, *is* to be taken literally. So my question is, how do you decide what is a literal command, and what's *not* to be followed?"

"Well, it's good to love enemies, but not good to mutilate yourself..."

"Um, yes, but the question still remains—why did Jesus say the command about chopping body parts if he didn't mean it?"

"He was just showing the seriousness of sin. That's all. That's all he meant."

"Hmmm. I wonder. It doesn't seem like the author of the book of Matthew would put commands such as 'go the extra mile, and don't be hypocritical or judgmental' side-by-side with 'chop off your arm if it causes you to sin' without specifically pointing out that one is supposed to be done literally and the other is merely figurative. That just doesn't make sense. There must be something else going on here. There's got to be a different way to understand this...Ah!" Chris exclaimed. "What about 'be perfect'? Isn't that in there, too? Doesn't Jesus command you to 'be *perfect*, as your father in heaven is perfect' (Matthew 5:48)? How's that going for you? Have you been perfect? Is that what you're striving for? To be *perfect*? (Matthew 19:21)"

"Yes, that's what the treadmill is for. I'm striving for perfection, just as Jesus commanded. I want to be perfect like Jesus. That is the goal. Religion was right, dammit! I've got to get back there...I've got to get back to my treadmill. So if you'll excuse me, I have to get back there before God is displeased..."

"But isn't that the reason Christ died on the cross, because we *can't* be perfect? That we fall far short?

"I've got to go..."

"No wait! Don't you see? Don't you see what's *really* going on here?" Chris said with excitement. "Jesus lived and taught *the* standard of perfection. The standard of perfection that is reflected in the Law of Moses. The 613 Laws of Moses. He said he didn't come to abolish the Law, but to *fulfill* it (Matthew 5:17). And with his red-letter words, he made it clear to us that it's unattainable. *All* of it! This tension was *meant* to drive people to the cross. To understand what the cross would mean. That Jesus was perfect in our place. He lived a perfect life *so we wouldn't have to.* There was never a need to parse things between what to follow literally and what is figurative. After the cross, Jesus had no intention of people trying to live and follow *any* of his red-letter words and teachings about the Law of Moses...he *knew* it was impossible, just as his friends and disciples were finding out when they were trying to live it with him. So why do people try to do that?"

Jesus-Follower thought for a moment. "Maybe because in Matthew 28 it says, 'teaching them all that I commanded you'....what about that?

"Hmmm, that's true. But why would Jesus contradict *himself*...hmmmm...I think there's a difference between the Law of Moses and Jesus's commands as he intended in Matthew 28. In the gospels, when Jesus teaches the Law, we are clearly told he is teaching Law. The writers clearly point this out. The Sermon on the Mount is all Law (and isn't just contained in chapters 5-7, but nearly the entire book of Matthew, since Jesus teaches the Law all the way through). It's introduced that way by Jesus himself! That means the narrow gate is the narrowness of *living the Law to perfection*—an impossibility! That is why he facetiously states that

35

'few will find it.' Thus the wide path of destruction is failing to be perfect under the Law, as your father in heaven is perfect—there is no way to attain it in our own human effort!...Let's see about some other passages...the log in the eyes—*LAW*...Do unto others as you would want done to you—a summation of the *LAW* and the prophets. Love your enemies—*LAW*...Love the Lord your God with all your heart, mind and soul and have no other god(s) before him—all *LAW*. The Ten Commandments...*obviously LAW*....The parable of the Good Samaritan is Jesus clarifying to a *law*yer how to live the LAW...it says so right in the text! And Matthew 18, the rich young ruler and parable of the unforgiving servant. All *LAW*. That is why the man is put in God's torture chamber. Because he doesn't live up to the perfection of the 613 Laws of Moses, which as James points out, 'guilty of one law, guilty of the whole Law.'" Chris took a breath. "So then we have Paul. Paul who says all people *no longer* live by the *LAW* (the written code), but by the *Spirit of God* (Romans 7:6)." Chris thought a moment. "So back to Matthew 28...maybe there are some commands of Jesus that have been overlooked...commands that *aren't* the 613 Laws of Moses...is that possible? Maybe we should explore that idea."

He sat down and read the Book for a few hours.

Jesus-Follower rested, enjoying the break from his striving (Psalm 46:10). He eventually fell asleep.

After a time, Chris woke him and said, "It's amazing. I've found a whole bunch of things Jesus commanded that no one ever emphasizes. Things we *should* do."

"What are they?" Jesus-Follower asked with excitement, for he really thought Jesus was incredibly cool and obviously had great respect for all he said and taught.

"Well, look at this: In Matthew 11:28-30, Jesus commands us to rest and not be burdened. And here...In Luke 10:38-42, Jesus tells Mary and Martha to cease from their working and serving Jesus to just hang out with him in enjoyment. In Matthew 9:15, Jesus says to celebrate now that the Messiah is here among you. And we know from the book of John through Acts that Jesus never leaves us. That is why the Holy Spirit came. I think Luke even intentionally put the story of the Good Samaritan (Law) back-to-back with the story of Mary and Martha resting with Jesus in enjoyment to clearly show the contrast between the Old and New covenants, as explained in detail in the book of Hebrews."

"You might be on to something here."

Chris smiled. Emboldened, he continued, "So here is a list of commands, *actual* commands of Jesus: Rest, hang out with God, enjoy God, celebrate that God is here. These words of Jesus are *not* part of him teaching the Law of Moses. In fact, he even goes out of his way to say in John, 'Here is a *new* command (as opposed to the Mosaic Law) that I give to you. That you love each other as I have loved you.' This saying is coupled with his announcement in John of the coming of the Holy Spirit after Jesus goes away. In the book of Acts there is a huge, wide berth of what it means to love others with the Holy Spirit present and active. Seems like something that goes on without the need for a written code (Romans 7:6).

"So yes, the Holy Spirit is described in the Book as being an ungraspable thing. Like wind (John 3:8) and freedom (2 Corinthians 3:17). Maybe people are just really uncomfortable with that? Seems too vague?...Seems too....ungraspable? Yes—A written list of rules is so much easier to follow, and more importantly, much easier to make sure *others* are following. So we try to live by a written code even though is goes directly against what the Book wants to communicate."

"Yes," said Jesus-Follower. "That seems a reasonable assessment. But I have a question: So if we don't follow the red-letter words of Jesus that are clearly the Law of Moses, then do we have no use for them? Should I just rip that part out of my Book?"

"No, I don't think that's necessary. I think they are still incredibly useful. With Jesus teaching the Law, we get a glimpse of how God interacted with a specific group of people at a specific time who were in a specific contractual agreement with him (Deut. 28). It seems to me there's a huge mine-wealth of meaning to glean from that, but it's not that *we today* are to follow the Law."

"Yes, that's good."

"Off the top of my head, here's just a tip of the iceberg of what we can learn: One, Jesus' interaction with those under the Law with him shows how far human nature is from the character of God, and two, since the Law is a reflection of the perfect character of God, a lot can be learned by considering what it says. It shows us that God is always forgiving, all the time. Always outwardly focused, all the time. Always putting others above himself, all the time, etc. It's God's nature in written code form. And if I want to consider what it means to love someone, I can think about these things. Not to follow them as expectations by God, or to live them to the letter, and certainly not to make sure others are living by them, but so that I might know what it means to love. Then I can love others in the way God uniquely made me. Not under the expectations of God (as if he'll turn his back on me if I don't), and certainly not to be a 'perfect' Law follower, and not even so I'll be 'Christlike' one day. Jesus rightly knew we weren't (and aren't) God, so it'd be foolish of God to expect us to try and 'be perfect.' That is why he went to the cross. To free us from written codes and laws of any sort between us and God. Paul said we are free, so we should live free (Galatians 5:1)."

"It's all starting to make sense now," Jesus-Follower said, smiling.

"Isn't it?" Chris replied happily. "I knew there must be some way to look at this that made logical sense between the words of Jesus and what Paul taught."

"I might have to change my name to 'Spirit-Follower.'"

"If you want. You're free to do so—or not. I'm not so sure it matters how we label ourselves, or don't label ourselves. Living free seems to be the most important thing, according to the Book."

"Agreed."

"As for me, my full name is Christian, not Chris. But I'm beginning to wonder if 'Christian' accurately describes me anymore. 'Christian' seems to be associated with the Book as religion—following Laws, rules, rituals and the red-letter words of Jesus. But I'm beginning to think that's not what the Book intended. I think it has more to do with freedom."

"Agreed again, my friend. You might be on to something there as well."

"But still, before I do anything rash, I'd like to check all this against what Freedom says. You know, just to be sure. Man, I sure wish he'd show up soon."

Chapter 7

The Pilgrim Descends Into Despondency....And Back Out

Then I saw in my dream that Spirit-Follower shook Chris' hand and gave him a quick hug.

He told Chris, "This has been excellent. I've really learned a lot. Now I'm off to wherever the Spirit leads. I can't wait to see what's in store for me. How exciting! Want to come?"

"I'll come and find you eventually," Chris answered. "I just want to wait a bit longer to see if Freedom comes back. I'd still like to discuss a few things with him."

And with that, Spirit-Follower took his leave.

Chris sat down to wait.

* * *

In time, two neighbors appeared on the horizon that lived in a miry bog out in the middle of the plains.

They should've built their houses on stilts, but they built them on gathered rocks instead, thinking it far better than 'sand.' (Stilts hadn't occurred to them, because it was never given as an option.) So their houses often flooded, causing them to pump water on a continual basis. Many of their possessions were tragically ruined.

The two men soon arrived and introduced themselves. One was called Christian Books. The other was called Biblical Motivational Speaking, aka, All Sermons, aka, Sermons.

Christian Books always dropped by to visit Chris on his treadmill to constantly nag him with criticisms of the church; how everyone is not doing 'it' right, how no one is committed enough, how everyone is not working hard enough, how everyone doesn't love Jesus enough, how everyone is always falling short, and how *he* (or she) has it figured out and is going to give *you* the lowdown on how to do *it* better.

Christian Books was unmarried and had no children. So no one was around to say anything otherwise.

And nobody thought to question it.

Biblical Motivational Speaking, aka, Sermons, began everything he said from the viewpoint that you as a believer are in a place, or state, that's not good enough. You're seriously lacking and/or displeasing to God as you are, and where you really need to get is somewhere else, someplace else, ie, you're *here*, but you need to get *there*...you need to be more like Jesus, or at the very least, you need to be a better version of you (because the one sitting in front of me sucks). Sermons always told everyone, "You're not good enough, you're not accepted enough, and dammit, you'd better not just sit there and rest! You need to *move*! You need to DO SOMETHING ABOUT IT! You suck as you are, and you need to change. You are Biblically mandated to change. It's called 'sanctification.' You must be better. You must not settle in and be comfortable. And I'm going to tell you how to change, how to move, how to be transformed..."

41

After all, it was his job to tell them this.

And ironically, everyone who listened to him paid him to say it.

When Christian Books and Sermons finally arrived, Chris was dismayed to see Religious was with them.

All three men nagged Chris harder than ever. After all, Chris was *still* standing still. He wasn't moving forward, so he *must* be moving backward.

And that simply could not stand.

So they nagged and nagged until Chris, under a ton of guilt and shame, became deeply despondent.

Their infernal nagging combined with Chris' already heavy burden of internal guilt and never-feeling-like-he-was-doing-enough-to-further-his-sanctification caused him to sink deeply in the dirt right where he stood.

Religious looked at him: "Ah, Chris. Where are you now? Looks like you're in a world of hurt if you ask me."

Chris, losing confidence in what he and Spirit-Follower had discovered, said, "Yeah, I don't understand it. I don't know where Freedom is. He should've been back by now....this is killing me! It's simply killing me! And you're not helping either, Religious. Not one bit."

Religious was offended and angrily chastised Chris. "Is this what that Freedom chap was telling you to do? Stand still and rest just so you can sink in the dirt? Look at you! This can't be good. I'm going back to my treadmill. If I can pull you out of this and onto your feet again, then a posh on that Freedom fellow! He's through! You can have him!"

With that, Religious plowed into Chris with a full football tackle, nearly breaking Chris' legs off, but it did nothing to help him budge.

He only sank further.

With a disgusted wave of his hand, Religious said, "I recommend you read the red-letter words in the Book and do what they say. Put them into action. They will get you out. That's my advice, it's the best I can do and I recommend you do it. I'm going back to my treadmill before I waste anymore time."

And with that, Christian Books, Sermons and Religion took their leave, feeling they had done their job.

Chris, confused that Freedom had seemingly abandoned him, did as Religious said. He grabbed the Book, studied the red-letter words of Jesus and even memorized some of them. He struggled and followed the red-letter words even *harder*, but got nowhere in gaining freedom from the position Christian Books and Sermons had put him in.

He only sunk further.

He had almost completely given up in despair when a neighbor he rarely saw walked up.

The man had military stripes on his sleeve and the number 3 on his front and the number 17 on his back.

Chris greeted him from deep in the dirt. "Howdy. I've seldom seen you around these parts. Are you in the military?"

"Yep. I'm in the 2nd Corps, special command to the King of this country. Say, why are you off your treadmill and stuck in the ground?"

"Oh, I got overburdened by a combination of cycles of personal guilt and confession and asking God for forgiveness, then trying harder than ever to be good—it's called sanctification—combined with the enormous pile of guilt and shame and never-doing-enough that Christian Books and Sermons put me under."

"Hmmm. I see. That's a drag."

"Yeah, it sucks. And what's worse, I got off my treadmill in the first place because some dork named Freedom said there was a better way. He talked me off the treadmill, told me to stay here then took off. Haven't seen him since."

"Maybe I can help," said 2nd Corps, with the 3 and 17 on his shirt. He reached out a hand to Chris and pulled him right out of the ground.

Easy as butter.

Chris felt greatly relieved. "Wow, 2nd Corps 3:17, thanks. I guess I should have been visiting you more often. Too bad we've been such strangers."

"Well, there's no need to keep calling on me or memorize my number. Just understand what I've done for you once and for all. It's really that simple. I hang out with Galatians 5:1 and Matthew 11:28 a lot...so if I were you," he paused and looked both ways, "if someone told you to stay here and wait in rest, that's what I'd do. Especially if it was someone important who said it."

Chris looked incredulous. "If it's all this easy, how come no one knows about this? How come *I* haven't been told about this?"

2nd Corps replied, "I'm not sure. But one thing I do know. This place is a mess. It greatly displeases the King seeing people living shackled under heavy burdens like this. People thinking they must be on a treadmill 24-hours a day. This is why he got rid of religion 2,000 years ago. To get rid of this very thing. And yet, this place may never be mended as long as Christian Books, Sermons, all paid clergy and the institutional church (which is really just a club/business) continues to exist in its present form.

Those things are like a machine. And the machine needs to be fed...and paid. The machine must continually teach that everyone and everything is in a state of 'not-good,' or incomplete, or deficient in some way so the machine can move them to betterment. They call it 'equipping the saints,' but it's really not right. It's nothing more than motivating people in your business to turn a 'profit.' The 'profit' is supposed to be 'spiritual growth,' so they teach things can never be good or right just as they are. Sermons constantly teaches, 'It is *not* finished,' contrary to what Jesus said, 'It *is* finished.' The horror of it all is quite clear: The machine needs to make sure people never perceive themselves as being good or righteous in their present state, even though Jesus made them this way by the cross. The machine can't have people thinking they've arrived. If that ever happened, the machine would collapse, and everyone would see it for the sham that it is."

"But isn't the 'church' also completing the mission Jesus gave in Matthew 28, The Great Commission? Isn't it all about saving souls as well as equipping the saints?"

"Those are good questions. And will be answered in time. But there's a better way to view the notion of 'salvation' in the Book, as well as The Great Commission. Don't worry, it will all come together in time. For now, in this present day and age as people are leaving the church in droves, there is a huge irony in play. Those who remain in church are lamenting the collapse of the machine, but its death will be the best thing for them.

"For everyone.

"For the whole world.

"For all of creation.

"And when the machine goes away (as more

and more people understand Freedom and rest), the Holy Spirit will have everyone in a better position to have the most fulfilled and abundant lives possible. Isn't this great? I think it's great. I'm excited. The process of the collapse and death of the machine might be painful for many, but it'll be a good thing in the long run. Trust me. A great thing. You'll see.

"So to sum up, mark my words: It is not the pleasure of the King to see people ensnared in the machine. It's a burdensome thing to him that this system should be so foul. The fact that the machine has made people feel like God's laborers—his slaves—2,000 years after he set them free, grieves him to no end. He did not send Jesus to the cross so everyone should shackle themselves to a religion called 'Christianity' propagated by a machine called 'the church.' There must be a rebellion! A rebellion led by Freedom. It's happening, and it's a wonderful gift to mankind. This is what God originally intended by his actions on the cross 2,000 years ago: For the world to be free from religion, religious machines and religious institutions. There is a better way, and that way is love. To simply love others."

"But love is not always so simple," Chris chimed in.

"Well, that is correct. But that is what community is for. Real community. True community. Not based on membership or those who are 'in' or 'out,' but people simply getting together to discuss how best to love each other and everyone on earth. How to create just economic systems, how to best preserve the environment and nature for the health of the planet and the enjoyment of future generations, etc, etc. Love has no boundaries. It's creative and growing. Abundant life is found wherever it is practiced. And it greatly pleases the

King. It's for this very reason he did all the work reconciling humans to himself. That we may be free to love and live life abundantly, doing things that are beneficial, not doing things that are harmful. It's really that simple."

Chapter 8

The Pilgrim and Freedom
Deep In Discussion

In my dream I saw that just as 2nd Corps 3:17 finished speaking and took his leave, Freedom came trotting over the horizon.

"Ah, good!" Chris exclaimed. "Just the man I wanted to see. It's been a wild ride since you've been gone, but I'm starting to figure some things out."

"Do tell."

"Well, first, a large man from the large town of Everything Outside the Christian Religion stopped to chat. In the course of talking, he tried to convince me to drag my treadmill and balance beam to his city and live there with them."

"What'd you say?"

"I turned him down. His offer for freedom was pretty good, but wasn't good enough. I needed a bit more."

"Yes, sounds about right. I know that man myself."

"Oh, you do?"

"Yes, I invite him to dinner now and then. Sometimes he comes. We have pretty good discussions."

"Hmm. That's good." Chris replied, happy that Freedom was already in the process of dialoguing with the man.

Freedom continued, "Yes, the main thing I keep trying to get him to see, along with those on the treadmills, is that the point of the Book is not that God is on the periphery trying to save people *out* of this world, but that God is front and center *in* this world healing and restoring it. There is no separation. There's no compartmentalization."

Chris thought this very wise, and very good news indeed.

Freedom asked, "So what else has happened?"

Chris excitedly related the things he and Jesus-Follower, now Spirit-Follower, discussed and discovered about Jesus.

"So do you think we were on the right track?" Chris asked after the summation.

"I think you figured it out exactly."

Chris grinned. "I knew it! I knew we had it right! It just made so much sense."

"Yes, that's what's been missing all these years in terms of seeming contradictions between Paul and the words of Jesus...well, been missing for centuries really."

"Seems so obvious now, but I guess I can understand why people have been so confused. After all, Jesus was God, and it doesn't seem a far stretch that if he was God, a religion would be built solely around him and his words. I guess people were too close to the trees to see the forest. You really have to step back and consider the context of the entirety of the Book to really see it."

"I agree. You've really been making some progress in lessening your burden, haven't you?"

"Yes, but it hasn't all been rosy since you left."

"Oh? How so?"

"Well, Christian Books and Sermons came

around and began berating me, and Religion was with them."

"Oh?"

"Yeah. Christian Books and Sermons successfully pounded me into a hole, and Religion was no help. Then a guy named 2nd Corps 3:17 came along and he made good sense. Right before he pulled me out of the hole, it dawned on me he was modeling 2 Corinthians 3:17. Spirit-Follower and I had discussed that verse earlier, but it was nice to see it in action."

Freedom nodded his head. "Yes, unfortunately Christian Books and Sermons make everything so complicated, but it's really quite simple. The Book is not 'life's little instruction book' to be lived and memorized every day. It's the communication of a truth: God conquered sin and death. And now we celebrate. It's really that simple."

Chris continued. "So yeah, overall I'd say I've learned a lot since you were away. So, anywho, let's get on with more instruction. I really want to finish well. That's my end-goal. I just want to finish well."

"Finish what?"

"My life. My walk with God. The purpose God has for me here on earth. You know, finish well. Paul said to finish the race, he buffeted his body into submission, he fought the good fight to win the prize...I want to finish well. Like Paul. I want to finish well."

Freedom looked at him. "I think we need to have a readjustment of what Paul was trying to accomplish and what he meant by all that. So let me ask you a few questions, and maybe we can unpack some misconceptions. First, let me ask you: Was Paul the first missionary?"

"Yes, of course he was. He set the standard.

Gave us the model. He planted churches all around the first century Roman world. I'd say that makes him the first missionary. He gave his heart, blood, soul and very life to see as many churches thriving in as many cities as he could before he died."

"He was trying to start something, I'll agree with that, but I'd argue his message was very different from how we think of it today. It *should* be the same message that we know, but it seems things have gotten a bit skewed over the centuries. But all is not lost. We can, and should, recover Paul's original message. Let's break it down and see if we can get to the heart of the matter and find out where things went wrong.

"Today, we think of religion, and what missionaries teach, as one choice among other choices. We chose which religion is true and we live it: Islam, Judaism, or Christianity, and then there's Hinduism, Buddhism, Shintoism, Mormonism, a million 'isms'....which to choose? That has always been the job of the missionary—to persuade people which religion is true, out of the many religious choices, and then live it."

"That's what Paul did, isn't it?"

"Well, not really. Paul simply took it upon himself to tell the world what Jesus did."

"That he died for our sins and now we can go to heaven, right?"

"Well, that, yes...but it's much, much more than that. Much more. For the Jews, the great news was this: You no longer have to live the Mosaic Law. The Law of Moses was no longer a binding contract between them and God now that Jesus rose from the dead. Jesus, on the cross, finished any outstanding business between humans and God—forever. It was *finished.* Now they were to live by the Spirit. And the

Spirit came in Acts chapter 2. Now God lives with humans as he intended in the Garden of Eden. But this time, instead of living *with* them, he lives *in* them. And in so doing, they can never get away from him ever again. He never has to 'cast them out of his presence' for anything they do, ever again.

"I want to repeat, because this is important: This relationship being held together is no longer dependant on *our* behavior (1 Tim 2:13). God lives *in* us so that he can always be true to *himself*, no matter what *we* do.

"So, yes, this was the great news for the Jews: Jesus died for their sins once and for all *and* they were now free from laws and contracts. God lived with them *freely*. There is no longer any standard of behavior to hold to. There was no longer any Deuteronomy 28 'you follow me and my rules, and you'll be blessed, and if not, you'll be cursed.' All that was done. Finished. Gone away. That was the good news, the *great news*, to the Jews. Now, when Paul came along, he wanted to give this same great news to the Gentiles (all-non Jews)—that God's kingdom had come to earth. Humans and God have been reconciled forever. And God never has to leave, or turn his back, on people because of evil ever again.

"In the book of Romans, Paul tells us some other important things. That yes, though the Gentiles were *never* under the Mosaic Law contract, they were still sinners with guilt before God (Romans 2:14, 3:23). But God took care of their sin-guilt with Jesus on the cross, just as he did for the Jews, so now *everyone* was free.

"But the Jews and Gentiles were not only free from sin, but free from the three other systems that made their lives miserable at that time: For Jews it

52

was the 613 Laws of Moses. For Gentiles it was pagan ritual evil. And for both of them, the oppression of the dark spirit world.

"So Jews lived under the burden of the Law of Moses, Gentiles didn't. Gentiles lived under the popularity of pagan ritual evil done for 'religious' reasons to either appease evil spirits, or just because bent human nature enjoys evil—ritual temple prostitution, etc. And Jews and Gentiles both lived under the oppression of evil spirits. Paul, being Jewish, often had mixed audiences of Jews and Gentiles as he went out to the cities with one goal in mind: To get people *free* from *all* those shackling systems—The Law of Moses, pagan ritual evil, and the oppression of evil spirits.

"These were the dominant shackling systems of *their* time. This was the contextual setting in which the New Testament letters were written. We don't have those systems hanging over our heads today. But *they* did. So Paul happily proclaimed that people were free from all of that now that the kingdom of God had come to earth through Jesus."

Chris was excited. "Yeah, and now that the kingdom of God is here, we have to be good, right? Because of course God's kingdom can't tolerate people being bad. So we need to be sanctif...."

"Hold on. No, that is not it at all. Paul makes it clear that since Jesus paid the penalty for sin, all *is* permissible, but not all is profitable (1 Corinthians 6:12, 10:23). He wanted people to know that since they were free, it wasn't wise to be evil (even though there was now no condemnation for it). So he persuaded them from logic to do what was beneficial to themselves and others, and not to live out the identity of the devil, which is sin, death and evil. John says 'the lust of the eye, the lust of the flesh,

53

and the boastful pride of life' characterizes the kingdom of Satan. That is the identity of Satan, *not* the identity of God's people. So don't align your lives with *that*, but live by the Spirit, Paul advises. Simply live with God, and do what is beneficial to yourself and others, and not what is harmful.

"This was Paul's simple message. There is now no longer a written code, or list of rules or standard of behavior that must be kept before God. God will never turn his back on you, and will always be *with* you and *for* you. But in your freedom, do *not* boast that you can do evil and God won't care (1 Corinthians 5). That is also an incorrect way to understand God's intentions.

"So to summarize: Paul was freeing people from the three dominant shackling systems of the day: The Law of Moses, ritual temple evil and fear of evil spirits. Now, I ask you, do you feel any pressure to fall back and live in bondage to any of those systems today?"

Chris thought about it for a second. "No. I guess not."

"You are correct. Those pressures don't even exist today. But this is what the bulk of Paul's words were about. He was trying to get people free from *those* things and persuade them to *stay* free. 'Be free' was his message (Galatians 5:1). Live in freedom with God, as originally pictured in Genesis 1 and 2. Simple as that."

Chapter 9

The Pilgrim Learns 'You Don't Have To Do That Anymore'

Chris looked thoughtful. "So let me see if I'm following you correctly. You're saying Paul never meant for us to go to church to 'practice our faith'? That he never meant Christianity to be one religious choice among other competing religious choices? That he simply meant for people to live *free.*"

"Yes. What it meant to Paul to 'believe' his message (to be a 'believer') was to be someone who knew there were no longer any requirements between humans and God in order to stay on God's good side. Even today, if we see someone doing *anything* they think needs to be done to appease God or keep him happy, we can gladly tell them the good news: That they no longer have to do that anymore.

"Today there is still an enormous amount of religion and superstition in the world. Sacred buildings where you have to take your shoes off because it's 'holy ground,' people who throw coins in certain areas of a temple to secure God's favor, or the favor of 'the gods.' People who go to church 'religiously' because God will be unhappy with them if they don't. We can gladly tell them the same thing Paul had the privilege to announce 2,000 years ago—*You don't have to do that anymore.* You *can,* in your freedom, do them if you want, but it won't change a single thing between you and God if you don't. And you shouldn't tell others they *have* to do those things for God either, because they simply don't.

"Paul makes the case several times in the New Testament that you lose your freedom if you go back to shackling yourselves under any system where you think anything you do, or don't do, keeps you on God's good side. Again, there is no condemnation for whatever you do, but it only makes sense to stay free, because God made you free. You shackle yourself once again if you 'believe' you have to do anything to keep God happy with you. So 'believe' the truth. Be a 'believer.' Believe you are free. Fight the good fight. Stay the course. Finish the race set before you. Stay free. Do not fall back into shackling systems. Your standing with God is secure, but in your everyday life, don't shackle yourself unnecessarily to religious or superstitious attitudes. Remain free. Fight the good fight to remain free with God. *That* is what Paul meant."

"So, back to the original point: Was Paul starting churches as we think of churches today? No, he was not. He was forming communities of free people who would support each other because living in freedom threatened the dominant systems of their day. It threatened the societal order of Jewish adherence to the Law of Moses and Gentile temple ritual evil. These systems were a matter of national security and oftentimes economic profitability, so many—especially those in leadership—persecuted those who didn't stay in line. Many 'Christians' were killed for opting out of those systems. (They were called 'Christians' not because it was a new religion, but because they were opting out of all shackling systems since Christ made them free). That is why the early church was persecuted. Not because Jesus was offensive. But because having people opt out for freedom was perceived as a threat to the social order.

"Think of Muslims converting from Islam today. Conversion, or opting out of Islam, threatens the stability of tribal society under the Koran (a form of unifying constitution.) It needs everyone to keep in line for it to work. Unifying tribes under Islam only works if everyone stays adherent to it. If someone wants out, it's a threat to national and societal security.

"There is a limit to American freedom as well. We are not *totally* free, in the outward sense. We are not free to commit treason (punishable by death). However, no matter where we live in the world, and no matter what system of government we live under, we can always be totally free in *ourselves*, in our deepest being, as God provided for us. That is the point of the Book. We are free—free of any and all kinds of religion, free from any outward shackling systems, free of our own internal sin-guilt and free from the oppression of bad circumstances we might find ourselves in at any given time. Free from it all because of what God did on the cross. And what God did on the cross only matters if we live free (James 2); free from shackling systems between us and God of *any* kind, be they religious, self-imposed, etc.

"So the perceived threat to the social order is why Paul and the early 'believers' faced persecution. But in the modern West, do we face these pressures today? No. Not at all. Actually, our political systems of freedom to a large degree mirror the fact that God set us free in our beings, in our souls. When God set humanity free, we've been progressing in this freedom as it works itself out individually *and* communally, such as in the writings of John Locke and Jean-Jacques Rousseau centuries ago.

"So again, we must ask ourselves, do we still need clubs and businesses (institutional churches) to keep us on the right path (to help us 'practice' our faith) because we are in danger of falling back into the Law of Moses or falling back into ritual temple pagan evil, or living in fear of the dark spirit world? Do we find these are problems for us today, especially in the West? No. They aren't. But they were *huge* problems for those in Paul's day, so he wrote about it and encouraged people to 'fight the good fight' to stay free. To finish the race of staying free.

"Again, to be a 'believer' in Paul's eyes meant to 'believe' Jesus made you free and you were no longer shackled under *anything* anymore. It was to believe that there were no longer any religious requirements or sacraments, or laws, or behaviors *of any kind* that God expected of you, and if you didn't, God would be displeased and/or turn his back on you. All of that was *finished* on the cross by Jesus, so now you are free. That is what Paul went around proclaiming. That's what he was so excited about. That's what he was willing to give his life for. But do we need to give our lives for it today? Or is the truth that Paul worked hard to push people away from those things, and he succeeded! (Again, at least as far as the West is concerned). And now there is nothing but our enjoyment of freedom in front of us.

"So I must ask you—today, do we need to do the job Paul was doing? Well, sure, if we see someone shackled under guilt or harmful addictions or superstitions who don't know Jesus made them free in their spirits—we have the privilege of telling them the news. And true, there may be some areas of the world that still need God's freedom proclaimed, but the West pretty much has no shackling religious systems holding people down, unless, of course, you count (ironically enough) the Christian Church. That can be pretty shackling. And it'd be good for people to know they are free from *any* religious shackling of *any* kind. Even the Christian kind."

"Ok, I hear you," Chris said. "I like it. This is good stuff. But I'm wondering: As far as 'church' goes, is there no use in us gathering together today? Can't we just gather together to talk about how cool God is?"

"Well, that's just it, isn't it? We don't 'practice our faith' as if we are on treadmills for God. But, yes, we can get together (though we don't have to) because we like God and the Book and Jesus and we want to love others. So maybe we can talk about ways to love others in greater ways, whether it's an environmental preservation project we're excited about and want to get others involved, or feeding the homeless, or educating immigrants, or teaching prisoners to read, etc. The point is we are free to be creative in love. And the future is not determined. There is no predetermined 'End Times' prophecies we are shackled under. There is no 'background grid' God has placed in history or in the universe that we are living against. The future is what we make it. We are free, like Adam and Eve originally in the garden, to shape the future and culture and make it what we want. And Paul advises us to take advantage of our freedom by partnering with God to make the world a better place—instead of a crappy place—for everyone."

"What you say makes sense. You've given me a lot to think about. It's good stuff so far."

"Well, I want you to sit here and rest some

more. I'm going to take another short break, then I'll be back and we can discuss many more things."

"Ok, but please don't be away as long as you were last time."

"I promise."

Freedom took his leave and Chris lay down in the grass once again.

Chapter 10

The Pilgrim Is Harassed By Evangelist

Then I saw in my dream that as Chris lay in peaceful slumber on the grass, a man ran up out of nowhere to inspect his state of being.

The fact that Chris was not on the treadmill caused the man great consternation. He shook Chris awake and yelled many things at him. Finally he barked, "Consider yourself warned!" and ran off.

His running was also motivated by the fact that Chris had picked up a large rock to throw at his head.

With the annoying man far off in the distance, Freedom arrived back on the scene. "Hello, Chris! Did you get some more sleep?"

"Well, sort of. For a little while I did, then this guy came by and shouted at me. Said his name was Evangelist. He shouted verses from the Book that seemed to be taken out of context. But I wasn't sure. They sounded really scary. I'm sure he was trying to scare me, so I wanted to chase him away before you arrived so I could have an undistracted conversation with you. I'd really like to know what the verses meant and maybe to understand why he shouted them at me."

"Ok, let's hear one."

"The first was Hebrews 12:25"

"Oh, Hebrews! I love the book of Hebrews. One

of my favorites."

"It is? But it seemed so...so...so...ominous."

"Naw, nothing in the book of Hebrews is ominous. I assure you. It's all great news. It just seems folks have highly misunderstood it through the years. Today it's so badly misinterpreted it seems to say nothing good at all. But I assure you, it's all good."

"Ok, enlighten me," Chris said. "The verse goes like this, 'See to it that you do not refuse him who speaks. If they did not escape when they refused him who warned them on earth, how much less will we, if we turn away from him who warns us from heaven?"

"Yes, very good. The warning is about turning away from freedom to go back into shackling religious systems—in this specific case, the Old Testament Mosaic Law with the accompanying animal sacrificial system.

"To unpack this, first understand that the book of Hebrews is one big argument for the fact that God—with the life, death, and resurrection of Jesus—has fulfilled and finished the Old Testament (the Law and the prophets and the sacrificial animal system).

"It's done.

"Finished.

"These things were fulfilled in Jesus and are no longer 'in play.'

"After Jesus rose from the dead, the only thing required by people is that they simply 'have faith' that God did these things. The audience of Hebrews simply needed to *believe*, without seeing (faith), that they no longer had to follow the Law of Moses (with the animal sacrificial system) to be right with God. They didn't need to continue doing sacrifices over and over as required by the Law of Moses. All they needed to do was *believe* those things were no longer necessary, and live in freedom from it.

"Faith is a one time thing. It isn't a process. Faith means knowing once and for all there isn't any outstanding work or deeds or rituals or law code of any kind that we have to adhere to in order for God to love us and not turn his back on us. In other words, to the audience of Hebrews, they were told they no longer had to live on the treadmill of Old Testament Laws, rules, or rituals.

"For us today, Hebrews means the same thing it meant to them—Jesus went through a lot to make you free. So live free. Don't fall back to believe any Old Testament requirements are still required. Don't fall back into believing any of your efforts or rituals are necessary to 'fix' anything between you and God. They aren't. Simply *believe* that God did all the work, and live in freedom. That's what faith is, and that's exactly what the book of Hebrews teaches. Every word of it.

"God takes freedom very seriously. He went through a lot to make you free. The author of Hebrews used strong language to convince its Jewish audience (hence 'Hebrews') that they were free. That they no longer needed to do the works of the Law nor practice the animal sacrificial system of the OT anymore, ever.

"Jesus fulfilled the law, and became a new law (Hebrews 7:12, 10:9). Jesus was the last sacrifice ever needed, so no more sacrifices need to be done. If we think more sacrifice is needed to fix anything between us and God, it renders what Jesus did useless (Hebrews 6:1-6). So live in the freedom that everything has been done. It's all been finished."

"Wow, I like that," Chris said. "It's nothing like what that guy was intending when he yelled at me. I never even knew that's what the book of Hebrews meant. I've heard so many different things, such as we have to live lives of constant faith or we displease God. So that's why we have to be on the treadmill and balance beam all the time. I was told it's a life of striving 'in faith' that God is with us and that our 'acts of faith' please him and if we don't do them we are displeasing to him. So we 'walk by faith' constantly, and not by sight. It's something we practice. Something we learn. It's a religion. A lifelong practice. It's called sanct..."

"If you say sanctification again, I'll scream. But yes, I think you understand now that it's none of that. We don't live 'faith' as an ongoing practice. We don't 'practice our faith' as some are keen to say. Faith is simply a one-time believing that the cross of Jesus made us free. All requirements between us and God were met by him on the cross. It's finished. We were *made* free so that we could *be* free (Galatians 5:1). Simple as that. So in the New Testament, the proof that anyone believed they'd been made free is that they *lived* free (James 2:14-19), no longer falling back into following Old Testament Law or rituals thinking those things made them 'right' with God or 'grew' them toward God. Those things simply were no longer needed *at all*. So James and Paul tells them, the evidence that you believe you've been made free is that you live free."

Chapter 11

The Pilgrim And Freedom
Continue The Discussion

In my dream, I saw Chris and Freedom continuing their discussion.

"I like what you're saying," Chris said. "Evangelist also yelled Hebrews 10:38 at me."

"Which says..."

"Which says, 'But my righteous one will live by faith. And I take no pleasure in the one who shrinks back.'"

"Yes, same thing. God went through a lot to fulfill the Old Testament Laws and Rituals to free the Hebrew people from all that. So he was telling them not to go back to the OT way of life now that they were free from it. It would make no sense. Same for us. Stay off treadmills. They are not necessary."

Chris looked confused. "But don't we get on treadmills out of gratitude for what God did for us on the cross? Out of respect and love for him? Isn't that a *good* thing?"

"No, it's actually the opposite. We stay *off* treadmills out of love and respect for God. He did everything. He doesn't need anything from us. We, in fact, are invited to partner with him in what *he* is doing, when we see *him* doing something. When the Holy Spirit lets us know there is something going on. And it's never burdensome or 'outside our comfort zones.' It's done in the power and plans of God. And if we don't want to partner with him in anything, we don't have to. Our standing, love and acceptance by God is sealed forever. God will always be *for* us and *with* us no matter what. It's especially not dependent on our behavior, actions or inaction. It all depended on what *he did* 2,000 years ago. That's all that matters."

"Hmmm. I think I'm beginning to get it. Ah, here was a strange one that guy yelled at me. He yelled, "'You are the man!' And I don't think it was because he thought I was cool or had done anything extraordinary."

"No, he was taking something from the Old Testament way out of context, which tends to happen a lot. He was trying to shame you into admitting your sin. This saying is from an incident that happened when Nathan was the prophet of God to King David. Nathan told a parable that exposed King David's adultery with Bathsheba and his subsequent murder of her husband after she got pregnant with David's baby."

Chris was excited. "Yes! God wants us to confess our sin, admit our failures, and then he will forgive us. He told David that what he requires is a 'humble and contrite heart.'"

"Well, the OT does say that what God wants is a humble and contrite heart. But those people lived under the Law of Moses, and were bound by its contract. But after Jesus, none of us are under the Law anymore, and as Gentiles, we never were. A humble and contrite heart was what God was looking for from people who were under the Law contract, which stipulated 'follow me and I'll bless you, don't follow me and I'll curse you.'

"But the book of Hebrews, as we just

66

discussed, is clear that Jews are no longer under the Mosaic Law contract, and Gentiles never were. So how do we relate to God after Jesus? By living in freedom, by understanding and believing in faith that God requires nothing from us. We don't have to confess sins to God. They are already forgiven. There is no 'growth toward God' happening in us in asking for forgiveness. We were forgiven everything 2,000 years ago. There is no process. There are no cycles of failure, repentance, have a contrite heart, ask God to forgive you, then go back out and try again. That kind of system was under the Law contract and because it was part of the Old Testament system, pastors and theologians have tended to blend it with the New Testament. But we are under a new system. A totally different system (Hebrews 7:11-19, 10:9). A system of freedom and complete forgiveness. Forever and for all time.

"Any sin I've ever done, or will ever do in my lifetime, is not retroactively forgiven by God on a moment to moment basis. It was all taken care of 2,000 years ago. We are now free. So live as free people Paul tells us in Galatians 5:1.

"Then in 1 Corinthians 6:12 and 10:23, Paul tells us, in your freedom 'do things that are beneficial, not harmful.' That is the only 'rule' we now live under. And we live under no condemnation (Romans 8:1). Ever. That's the craziness of the risk God took by Jesus dying and raising from the cross 2,000 years ago. He took away the sin of the world. Forever. And since then, the human race has been free. Totally free."

"So how does God deal with evil and harm and victims of injustice and stuff like that?"

"In his own wisdom, knowledge and understanding. We simply have to trust that he knows what he's doing."

"Does that mean we shouldn't put anyone in jail or punish anyone for a crime?"

"Not at all. When we do wrong, it still affects us and those around us with negative consequences. The difference is, in relation to people toward God, God doesn't have to retreat from the scene or 'cast anyone from his presence' ever again because of sin. This was dealt with by Jesus on the cross. The sin barrier was destroyed, nullified, ended forever. It means God can stay with us no matter what, as the power of what Jesus started on the cross continues to be worked out in the healing and restoration of all creation.

"And we (all humans) are invited to participate and partner with God in this healing and restoration. In God's power, God's energy, God's timing and according to God's plans—not ours. We are at rest and at peace in our souls. We do not have to be on any treadmills. God takes us for a ride of abundant life and mind-blowing activities as we see him reversing the effects of sin in the world, to the point where there will eventually be no physical death on earth at all (1 Corinthians 15:25-26)."

"Might be an overpopulation problem at that point."

"Ha, yes, I'm sure. But I'm thinking God's thought that one through and has made arrangements for it."

"Yes, I guess you're right."

"Ok, anything else he yelled at you from the Book?"

"Basically, he lastly told me I was rejecting Jesus."

"Huh. Well, to 'believe' in Jesus in the NT sense is to *not* live under any shackling religious systems of any kind.

"Paul, John the Baptist and the NT writers were *not* announcing a new religion. They were announcing the coming of the Jewish Messiah and what that meant for the world. It was most certainly not a 'split off from Judaism' or an 'emergence from Judaism.' Nor was it an end to Judaism so that Christianity may compete alongside it as another religious choice.

"It's important we understand this: Judaism pointed the way to Christ, but Christ was not starting something called 'Christianity.' He never meant to do that. Christ was the fulfillment of the Old Testament scripture and the end of the way of anyone relating to God through a written code (rules and rituals) and animal sacrifice.

"Contrary to popular belief, the NT doesn't tell us to live a new religion, or how to live a new religion. It simply communicates that Jesus fulfilled the Judaic scriptures (1 Corinthians 15:3-4). Jesus is not a way of life. Jesus's life and death communicated a truth. That the sin barrier, and any outstanding business between man and God that needs 'paid for' has been finished and done.

"Done.

"Finished.

"The transaction is complete.

"There is nothing else that needs to be done."

Chapter 12

The Pilgrim Learns Life With God Is Easy And Light

Freedom continued: "It's unfortunate, but as we showed earlier, people have succeeded in making Jesus a religion. This religion is an offshoot of Judaism called 'Christianity.'

"It developed because people thought Jesus came to have everyone follow his words and teachings. But as we discussed earlier, Jesus didn't intend that. He was teaching the 613 Laws of Moses to those who were under the Law with him (Galatians 4:4), because he was fulfilling it. He was teaching them how to live the Law correctly and as exactly and as perfectly as God required, and as required of them by the Deut. 28 contract. And in his having lived the Law perfectly, Jesus showed how impossible it was for any human to do it, thus, it pointed to the fact that his sacrifice on the cross was needed (as foreshadowed in Hebrew culture by animal sacrifice).

"Jesus sacrificed himself *in our place.* And Paul says this act was *not* so we could live a new religion, but so that we could be free (Galatians 5:1). Free from religion. Free from anything shackling us in a spiritual or religious way. Jesus was never meant to be lived as a religion.

"And Paul, and the New Testament writers, spent most of their time arguing that being free didn't mean that God now condones evil if we choose to practice evil (1 Corinthians 5). No, that's not what God had in mind. Evil is not the identity of the spirit of God, Peter and John argue in their books. Love is. Evil is the identity of Satan and the demons.

"So, Paul says, do not use your freedom as an opportunity for evil, but for love (Galatians 5:13). In your freedom, partner with God in the restoration and healing of creation. This is where life will be found. This is where abundant life is found. (But you don't *have* to—you can do nothing if you wish and God will still be *for* you and *with* you. Forever.)

"So churches should not be a place where people 'live the Christian life' on treadmills. In fact, churches and Christianity as it's known today should be ended and go away.

"What should take its place are groups of people who get together who want to understand and take part in what God is doing to restore and heal creation through love. We can get together and discuss how to improve life on earth. How to create global economic systems that are more just. How to end racism, fear, corruption and poverty. How to give all people on earth a greater sense of security so war will end. In this way, God will eventually rule the earth, because he is with us as we participate in these things. God is directing the show. Fueling the energy to do it.

"It's not in our power or energy or plans. But in God's power and energy and plans. And another tremendous benefit of this process (much like the very, very, very slow processes observed in the physical sciences and evolution) is that sin and death will be slowly eradicated from the human race, entirely, until even physical death itself no longer exists (Revelation 21 and 22, 1 Corinthians 15:25-

26).

"Anyone not willing to go in this direction will simply lose out. They will not be in eternal hell, necessarily, but they will not experience life, and life to the fullest."

Chris rubbed his chin. "So how exactly does God deal with those who choose evil instead of love?"

"It's up to him. In Matthew 13 Jesus says to trust in God's sense of justice and fairness (Matthew 13:24-30, Revelation 21:26-27). He sees all and can deal with it. But from the rest of the Book, we see that God pretty much leaves free-will up to us to decide the direction we go in life, and how we experience it. If we choose to abuse others, God will deal with that.

"But if we choose love, we will experience 'eternal life;' life to the fullest, abundant life. He communicates in the Book that the best way to live is to love others and always move toward the healing and restoration of everything, and if we go against that and choose to practice evil, it's to our detriment and the harm of others on earth. He doesn't need to 'throw' anyone into hell. Your experience of your existence is in your hands. But Paul and the NT writers argue in heavily logical and persuasive ways that love is the best way to live. So choose love. It's the most fulfilling, most abundant, most satisfying and exciting way to live.

"I don't think it takes rocket science to grasp that love is better than evil. John says 'God is love.' (1 John 4:8). Not that love is God, but that love is the overwhelmingly dominant characteristic of God. We are free. We can live in our identities as children of God. We are part of God's family, and at the top of our family tree is love. That is who we are. That is our family line. That is who we were made to be. So in your freedom, Paul says, choose love. No one is cracking the whip beneath you. No one requires you to live on a treadmill.

"Rest.

"Relax.

"Be free.

"Live with God.

"It's *easy*.

"It's *light*.

"And it's worth it.

"Because love is the direction God is going.

"And it always will be."

Chapter 13

The Pilgrim Gains Clarification

"Ok," Chris said, "I have a question."

"Let's hear it," Freedom answered.

"The book of Hebrews tells us the communal animal sacrificial system as mandated in the Old Testament is no longer needed, but what about sacrifices to God in our individual lives? Doesn't Romans 12:1 tell us to 'present ourselves as living sacrifices to God'?"

"Well," Freedom started, "that one verse is probably most responsible for people thinking they need to live on treadmills; thinking they have to do things for God to please him; thinking that working and striving to 'serve God' is our way of showing our gratitude to God for dying for us on the cross. So we think we must make ourselves 'a holy sacrifice, acceptable and pleasing to God.' However, this has nothing to do with the actual context of these verses. And what's most responsible for causing this problem is the arbitrary chapter break between Romans 11 and 12.

"The overall goal of the book of Romans was the same as Paul's goal for most of his NT letters: To unify two groups who were historically disunified: Jews and Gentiles. Paul wanted to communicate to *both* sides that God is now with them *all*, so they could now *all* live together in *love*, under the freedom they received when Jesus set all humans free.

"So in Romans, we have two groups: Jews and

74

Gentiles. And, in their freedom, both groups were still quarrelling. The lead-in from the end of chapter 11 is Paul discussing that each side is harboring an arrogant attitude of God's favoritism. The Jews were claiming they were better because they were the original 'chosen people' of God with the Law, the temple and all the OT trappings, while the Gentiles were feeling superior because the Jewish people had largely rejected Jesus, so God now favored the Gentiles.

"First, interestingly, Paul affirms *both* positions. He says, yes, the Jews were special because God did historically work primarily through their culture. And that was a good thing. And that yes, the Gentiles are now special because Gentiles were benefiting from what the Jews largely rejected— freedom in Christ. *But*, Paul states, eventually both sides will be *equally* special and *equally* favored by God as the one, unified 'new Israel.' So tune yourselves into that truth now, *sacrifice* your arrogant attitudes, and get along with each other. That is what Paul means in Romans 12:1. With these statements, he plays on Old Testament sacrificial system language.

"How do we know this interpretation of 12:1 is correct? Well, you'll notice that Romans 12:3 continues the discussion from chapter 11 of both sides being arrogant about their 'favored' status before God. In 12:3, Paul says, 'do not think more highly of yourselves that you ought, but be humble (think of yourselves exactly as God sees you).' We see that Romans 12:3 is a continuation—indeed, the conclusion—to Romans 11. Therefore, 12:1-2 must be *within the context* of laying down, of *sacrificing*, their arrogant attitudes toward each other.

"In conclusion, with the unfortunate chapter

break between Romans 11 and 12, theologians have unwittingly completely pulled Romans 12:1-2 out of context to mean something never intended by Paul."

Chris: "Ok, what about Hebrews 12, which states God disciplines us for our betterment? And to shirk off the sin that so easily entangles us to better live the life God wants us to live?....what about those?"

"Ok, one at a time. First, the notion that God disciplines us, the common interpretation of Hebrews 12: This is actually not about God disciplining *us*. The audience of this book was forsaking their freedom in Christ and falling back into OT ritual and Law. The author of Hebrews was strongly chastising them for doing that. The author was warning them not to do it. The author was, in effect, publicly embarrassing them for doing the wrong thing. And in a shame-based culture, this was devastating. So the author was pointing out that God was not *punishing* them, he was *disciplining* them for their good. God worked hard to make them free, so the author of Hebrews wanted them to keep from falling back into shackling themselves once more under OT Law and ritual.

"This discipline has nothing to do with *us*. It was important that those early believers opting for freedom not mix rules and rituals into the freedom God meant for the world. If the mixture was permitted to continue, then freedom would no longer be visible. Freedom would no longer exist. And God worked hard from the cross to give us freedom.

"Fortunately for us, the NT letters had their effect. We are free. We are no longer communally pressured to follow the 613 Laws of Moses. (Though some still choose to shackle themselves with it, unfortunately. And I'm talking Christians here, not

76

just Jews).

"Ok, Second. The 'sin' that so easily entangles us in Hebrews 12:1. This verse is not about 'doing bad things.' No. The sin that entangles is falling back into Old Testament rules and rituals, thinking those are necessary in relation to God, as if there is still unfinished work between humans and God. That is the 'sin' the author of Hebrews is telling them to let go of.

"'Sin' as a word describing falling back into a non-free Law and ritual based way of relating to God is also used in James 5:20 where he says, 'Remember this: Whoever turns a sinner (someone opting for law and ritual over freedom) from the error of his ways will save him from death and cover over a multitude of sins ('sins' here being the effects of leading people astray from freedom—ie, false teachers).' The false teachers were leading people into sin (sin= that which goes against the will of God) in leading people back into an OT system God declared (by the cross) that they were no longer under. With this sentence, James is indicting the rich religious members of the community who were pressuring and persecuting and 'teaching' or advising those in 'freedom' to fall back into OT law and ritual.

"James (and Hebrews) make it clear that falling away from freedom only leads back to a life of shackling death, in essence rendering Jesus's work on the cross null and void, as if it never happened, something which is contrary to the will of God after the cross. We simply have to 'believe' (have faith) that it's true that Jesus did everything, and now there is nothing outstanding in terms of anything more that needs to be done between humans and God. We show that we believe this by *not* believing

77

that we still must do things for God and if we don't, he will be displeased.

"God did the work. It's done. It's true, and it's there. Jesus death and resurrection from the cross was set in stone 2,000 years ago. All we need to do is understand that it's there. And believe all was finished *at that time*. We don't show we believe it by being or becoming religious, or living or becoming 'Christian.' A show of outward works is not necessary (an historically damaging mis-interpretation of James 2). We show we believe it by living free of *all* religious systems, and living free of *all* religious fear.

We show we believe it by living free (James 2).

Chapter 14

The Pilgrim And Freedom Clear Up More Mess From Evangelist

Chris seemed satisfied with the explanations Freedom gave him.

"I like what you're saying," Chris said. "The guy also told me this little gem: 'Galatians 6:12: Those who want to impress people by means of the flesh are trying to compel you to be circumcised. The only reason they do this is to avoid being persecuted for the cross of Christ.' I think he was trying to say I was lame."

"Well," Freedom replied, "this verse is not about you being lame. I can assure you that. This is not about people in our day making an outward show of religion just so they won't be persecuted for Jesus. It's about people in *that time period* making an outward show of religion so they wouldn't be persecuted for being free of all religious, ritualistic and superstitious systems of *their* day.

"Again, *today*, we don't have anyone pressuring us to follow the Law of Moses. At that time, they did. There was a heavy top-to-bottom societal pressure to do this, because it was the dominant religious/political system of the day and anyone opting out by choosing freedom in Christ was persecuted because they were seen as being a threat to the stability of society.

"This threat does not exist for us today in The

West. No one that I know of is being threatened or pressured to live under the Law of Moses. We couldn't follow most of the Law even if we wanted to. The Law involved very specific things like 'Give your donkey a rest from its work on the seventh day (Exodus 23:12).' How many of us today own donkeys? Not many. This is probably one reason why God had a *specific* group of people follow it for a *specific* period of time. That time has passed. The people of that lineage are now free, just like the rest of us. So today, we shouldn't invent persecution that isn't there."

Chris chimed in, "Some today interpret this verse to be about 'pew-sitters' who think they are going to heaven but haven't done the hard work of 'putting their lives on the line' for Jesus, so they are just fooling around and will end up in Hell. What about that?"

"Well, the text doesn't allow us to make that jump. That would be ridiculous in the mind of Paul. Paul would be glad for us today that, at least in America, we don't live in a country where religious pressure is bearing down on us. If anything, sadly and ironically, people who *aren't* Christian may feel religious pressure from Christians and Christianity. Paul would think this a travesty of the highest order, no doubt. It would grieve him greatly. But he would love that we live in religious and political freedom. He would be amazed and astounded and greatly happy for us."

With this, Freedom decided to take another break and took his leave, but not before advising Chris to sit down and rest, and wait for him to get back.

No sooner had Freedom gone than Evangelist came back.

"Oh...you again." Chris said blandly.

"Yes, it's me. And unawares to you, I didn't completely leave the last time we spoke but merely ran away a bit, turned and came back. I was hiding over there next to your house in the bushes all this time."

"That's not creepy at all," Chris said with sarcasm.

"Creepy? Maybe so my good man, but I did it for your protection."

"Huh? My protection?"

"Yes, from that Freedom fellow. He's all wrong. I would advise you not to listen to him. There are things he said you should absolutely abhor, and I will list them for you now."

"Great..." Chris said with more sarcasm.

"First—His persistent insistence that you stay off the treadmill. That is a lie and the work of the Devil. The treadmill is a good thing and we must all stay on it. Second—Him trying to say that 'pew sitters' are not in the danger of Hell, because they are. The cross is an offense to them. They must try harder and get up off their asses and onto their treadmills if they want to avoid the fires of the damned. And third—I might point out that him getting you off the treadmill has set your feet toward the hells of death. You need to constantly sift what you hear against the truths contained in the Book. Always be on your guard, always on edge, and never, ever relax! Untrue philosophies of men are creeping up everywhere to attack you! They will make you fall off the balance beam and God will be displeased. So be on alert! Your adversary the Devil is always looking for someone to devour!"

And he made the same claw hands Mr. Worldly-Wise had made. He made the same noise—

growl!—only this time there was no chuckling or sense of silliness to it.

He was deadly serious.

Evangelist continued his tirade. "In addition to this, your sin is very great! In fact, it's twofold: First, you got off the treadmill, and B, you're listening to what that fool Freedom is telling you. So stop! Or you will burn! Get back on the treadmill and don't deviate from the path so that you will be received when you reach The King. It is a narrow road you must go. So get back on it! Ok, that is all. Have a good day."

"But....how will I ever get to the King using the treadmill? I don't seem to be getting any closer to..."

Chris wanted a bit more information and discussion, but Evangelist felt his job was done, so he left.

Huh, Chris thought. *That was hugely unhelpful...*

And he lay back down and fell asleep.

Chapter 15

The Pilgrim Joins The Party

After a while, Chris awoke to see a group of people hanging lights, installing a sound system, and setting-up a table spread with all manner of good food and drink.

Someone hung a banner over the whole area that said, "Knock, and it shall be open to you."

It was all the work of one man, who was still busy getting things ready.

Chris called to him. "Hey, there! How's it going?"

"Great! Things are good!"

"Who are you?"

"Oh, sorry," the man walked over and shook Chris' hand. "My name's Goodtimes. How are you?"

"I'm well rested, thank you very much. Haven't felt this good in years."

"Then you'll have lots of energy for the party."

"Party? What are we going to celebrate?"

"Life, the universe, and everything! Isn't it great?"

"Ok, sounds fun. I'd like to join the party. How much does it cost?"

"It's free."

"Free? But you've been putting up all this stuff..."

"No problem, man. It's been paid for. Time to celebrate!"

Chris looked off in the distance. "Hmmm.

Shouldn't we put up a shield or something? Those little red fellows up on the hill look like they might want to shoot arrows at us."

"Naw, they can't touch us. Can't shoot that far. Non-factor."

"Ok, well I should at least help you do some work."

The man quickly pulled a couch from nowhere and had Chris sit down.

"There you go."

"You mean I don't have to do anything?"

"It's already been done. We're ready. Just waiting for other guests to arrive. Don't you have anyone else with you?"

Chris turned and whistled loudly. His wife and children came out of the house and joined the party.

"Is there anyone else?" Goodtimes asked.

"Well, Religious left a long time ago to go back to his treadmill. And if Christian Books and Sermons don't drastically change their tune I don't think they'll ever be in good enough shape to attend the party. Not sure if Mr. Worldly-Wise would want to come, but I'll give him a call. Can't stand that Evangelist fellow...wouldn't want him here anyway, unless he drastically changed as well and decided to stop yelling and misquoting the Book."

"So none of the others want to lay down their difficulties and join the party?"

"I guess not."

"Seems foolish to me, but hey, they can do what they want. We all live in freedom."

"I have to admit, I was tempted to go back to my treadmill several times, but in the end, I'm glad Evangelist was a jerk and yelled stuff at me because the ensuing discussion I had with Freedom was more valuable than gold."

"I'll say. That Freedom guy is great. Knows what he's talking about. I enjoy hanging out with him."

"So who's coming to the party? Were invitations sent out?"

"Yep. Everyone in the entire world who wants to come can come. We have no 'A' list, no roster of guests. Invitations are sent out continually. Every second of the day, in fact. Everyone gets one. Anyone can come to the party any time they simply want to shed their burdens and be free. And they can come and go as they please, but seems this is better than most other choices I've seen out there."

"Looks good to me. I'm going to get some food."

Chris got off the couch and went to the food table. He came back with a plate stacked high with delicious treats.

"Stick here with me," Goodtimes said to Chris as he turned on some music, "and we'll have some fun. Look over there!"

Chris turned and saw the Patriarchs, the Prophets, Christ and His Apostles smashing Chris' treadmill and balance beam with large axes.

"Wow! Where'd they come from?" Chris exclaimed, then looked downcast. "I can't believe I used to live like that. Thinking everything was so narrow. That there was a line I had to walk, not going to the right or left but always on a pencil-thin edge without falling off. I thought moving to the left or right was full of dangers and that I would lose my way and be entrapped if I didn't continually drive myself toward my purpose with God. And if I didn't, horrible things would happen."

"But none of that is true. Feels good to know that now, right?"

"I'll say," Chris brightened up. "Hey, is there

anything at this party that might ensnare me? Any twists or turns I won't see coming that will make me lose my way?"

"Nope. Nothing at all. You can relax. Just chill."

"You mean I'm all done with spiritual worry and strife and not being good enough and always having to do more, always having to do better, to be better, and always going uphill, driving and striving and working in sanctification to perfect myself so I'll one day be 'Christlike'?"

"Ok, boy. Stop. Just stop. Yes, all that is done. God is here at the party with you. Celebrating. That is all that is left to do now. He took care of everything else. Just chill."

"You say God is here? Where?"

"Right over there."

"No way!"

"Way!"

"There he is! Right over there! Wow," Chris took a deep breath. "It may take a while for all this to sink in, but for now I'm going to get more of that awesome cheese dip."

"Godspeed with the cheese dip."

Chapter 16

The Pilgrim Is Kidnapped
From The Party

Next I saw in my dream that after a time of fun and celebration, two men approached Chris at the party and kidnapped him.

He kicked and struggled, but they threw a bag over his head and carried him away.

Eventually Chris felt himself being seated in a chair. The bag was lifted from his head and he saw he was in a house. All around the room folks were on treadmills, working away and sweating profusely.

Pastor Hard Work and Sermons was seated directly in front of him.

"Hello, Chris," Sermons greeted him.

"Oh, hey," Chris said half-heartedly. "Kidnapping is a crime, you know."

"That was for your own good," Pastor Work replied. "We needed to get you back on track, young man. No more celebrations and such kinds of nonsense. Such a waste of time and money (John 12:1-8)."

"Seemed like a good thing to me."

"But, I'm sorry to say, it's not supported by the Book. The Book clearly states in Galatians 4:19-20, 'My dear children, for whom I am again in the pains of childbirth *until Christ is formed in you*, how I wish I could be with you now and change my tone, because I am perplexed about you!' Here, clearly,

Paul is talking about 'sanctification.' Your treadmill. That you need to work toward your 'Christlikeness.' You need to progress toward having Christ formed in you. That's what he said. It's your job. For the rest of your life."

"Hmmm. Not so sure about that..."

Fortunately for Chris, and unbeknownst to the others, Freedom had given Chris an earpiece in case he was ever taken to the place he now found himself; the house of Questionable Interpretation. The earpiece actually allowed Freedom to hear what was being said so he could respond to Chris right away.

Freedom's voice crackled: "*Remember, Paul's goal in the New Testament was to get people completely clear of Old Testament Law and ritual. The book of Galatians was written to folks who were struggling with falling back into mixing the freedom Christ gave them with OT Law and ritual. Circumcision as a religious requirement was one aspect of the Mosaic Law hotly debated among the Galatians. What this verse actually means is that Paul is looking forward to the day when they will be totally free and clear of all OT Laws and Rituals, and the freedom Christ gave them will be all that's left. Christ will then be formed in them; that Christ's work on their behalf will be all there is, and OT Law and Ritual will once and for all be a non-factor.*"

"Makes sense," Chris muttered.

"What's that?" Pastor Work asked, startled.

"Nothing," Chris replied. "Can I go back to the party now? You guys can't legally keep me here."

"Boy!" Sermons roared. "Have you not been listening to anything we've been saying? Do I have to repeat myself over and over again until you do what I say? Because I will! I'll tell you the same thing week after week until you start doing it...Oh! I swear the church is in such bad shape these days. Everything is going to Hell in a handbasket!"

"But at least I'll enjoy the ride," Chris snickered.

"Boy! Again! This is no joking matter!"

"I wasn't joking."

"That's a terrible attitude!" Pastor Work huffed. "God loves the church, and so should you!"

"The church? You mean what's going on here with all these people on treadmills and sweating and suffering and stuff? You think God is *here*, with them? That's interesting, because I just saw God over at the party and…"

"Blasphemous!" Pastor Work shouted. "If it weren't for the fact we're trying so hard to save you, we'd have to kill you!"

Chris just stared at him.

"We must get to work clearing all the corruption from your heart. Jesus started it all, yes, but there is much to be dug out from your cruel and evil heart. It will be a long, drawn out and painful process. Like a nasty surgery where you've been given no anesthesia. But we can, and will, build you another treadmill and balance beam so you can get started once again."

Chris was getting agitated. "Can I go back to the party now? I'd really rather do that. There's people there I'd like to see…"

"No you can't! There is no party! (Luke 15:22-24; Matthew 22:1-4; Matthew 25:10) And the sooner you get that through your head, the better! You must get to work cleaning yourself up; you must be like Christ!" (Galatians 3:3)

Chris was so exasperated at this point he felt he was going to die.

And Christian Books stood silently in the back

of the room nodding his approval.

Chapter 17

The Pilgrim Endures Interrogation

"I don't need to clean myself up," Chris told them. "My heart and soul are already clean. God made me a 'new creation.' How can a new creation be stained? Why would God make me new, and then let sin still be there? That makes no sense."

"Are you saying you're perfect now?" Pastor Work bellowed. "That you don't do anything wrong? That you are exactly like Christ?"

"First of all, I still sin, yes, but sin doesn't live in me (Romans 6). Second, I don't have to become exactly like Christ. Christ lives in me, so I can be me and he can be him (Galatians 2:20). I hardly think he wants us to become God. I am happy being the finite, limited me with God's spirit living in me. God can stay God. I can stay me. It's a good arrangement."

"But what about sin? That's what we're getting at."

"Well, I no longer have a sin nature. I'm not controlled by sin (Romans 6). I can renew my mind—simply think about things differently. I used to live in the land of 'sin' but I have a new passport. I can't go back to being a citizen of 'sin' because God gave me a new citizenship (Romans 6). Now I can do things that are beneficial, and not do things that are harmful. No big deal, really. You guys seem to make such a big deal of 'sin.' Didn't Christ take care of that on the cross so we don't have to focus on it? Why do you guys make sin/not sinning the primary focus of your lives? That doesn't seem to be the point of the Book at all."

"Not focus on 'sin'!?" everyone in the room gasped. That is, everyone except Chris, who now had a look of perfect serenity on his face.

"But sin must be conquered!" Sermons snapped.

"Sin has *already* been conquered!" Chris snapped back. "Haven't you read the Book? You can borrow mine if you want."

Sermons smacked his own forehead. "But a sinner cannot enter the kingdom of God!"

"I know!" Chris answered. "I'm not a sinner. Yes, I sin now and then. But I'm not a sinner by nature or identity. I'm a new creation. I have a new identity. And it's not 'sinner.' It's child of God and heir of the King."

Pastor Work looked deflated. "I see we're getting nowhere with this," he sighed. So he changed gears and took a different tack. "About this party and celebration business. Don't you know that that stuff doesn't happen in *this* life? It's supposed to be delayed until the next life. In *this* life, we live and strive in misery for God as we cleanse ourselves of all unrighteousness, then we're rewarded greatly in the next life for how hard we worked to make ourselves 'good' (Galatians 3:3). Don't you know that the *next* life is when the fun, party and celebration begins? Isn't that what you were taught?"

"Well, it's what I was taught, but I think there's a better, more accurate way to see things. Would you like me to explain what's in the Book? I can interpret it for you if you like."

Naturally, this infuriated them. "You cannot,

and *will not*, tell us what to do! We're professionals! You certainly won't tell us what's in the Book! We know damn well what's in there! And the truth is that we, the people of the Book, will get all good things in the *next* life if we sacrifice everything in *this* life. The crappier we make this life for ourselves the better the next life will be for us. It's that simple. Those in Everything Outside the Christian Religion are having their fun now, but they'll get nothing but rags and crap to eat later! That's the deal!"

"And that makes you *happy*?" Chris asked incredulously. "That all those other people will get rags and crap to eat later? That seems pretty sick to me."

"It's not!" Sermons snapped. "It's loving and good! It's the way things are. The first will be last and the last will be first. That's what Jesus said."

"Hmmm. Loving...yeah, right."

In his ear, Chris heard Freedom say: "*The 'last and first' thing from Jesus was actually Jesus giving a warning to some of the Jews who were under the Law with him. These folks had the idea they were the best and most favored of God and were therefore going to get all good things from God automatically as 'children of Abraham' while others (the Gentiles, the non-Law following Jews, the 'dogs') would get little or nothing in the end. Jesus warned them to watch out, because a new system was coming—nothing less than the Kingdom of God itself—where everything was turned on its head and* all *were welcome. That's what the Jewish Messiah, Jesus, was going to do for everyone. For all people. So actually, the ones thought to be 'last' were actually going to be 'first' in God's economy. This Jews-Gentiles tension has nothing to do with us today.*"

"Ok, thanks," Chris said.

"What?" Sermons snapped. "Why do you keep mumbling to yourself?"

"None of your business." Chris got up. "Well, this has been fun, boys, it really has, but I've got to get back to the party. There's probably been a lot more people who've shown up since you brought me here—against my will I might add—and I'd like to get back and see them."

Just then, Chris thought he heard a loud noise, like the jangling of heavy chains, coming from a room below. "What was that?"

Pastor Work and Sermons looked at each other. Christian Books moved toward the center of the room.

"That's something we were hoping to spare you of."

"What?"

The three men collapsed in the middle of the room for a huddled whisper.

Pastor Work eventually announced, "Yes, ok. Maybe it's for his best."

"What's for my best?" Chris asked.

Pastor Work sighed. "We were hoping to keep this from you. We were hoping you'd come to your senses and listen to us, but now—seems we have no choice."

"Jesus, fellas! What are you going to do to me?"

Chris was terribly frightened.

"It's not what we're going to do to you, it's what becomes of anyone who opts off the treadmill. It happens naturally, I'm afraid. As outlined in the Book."

Chris was terribly confused, but followed the three men into the basement where a smallish iron cage sat in the middle of the room.

A bent and gnarled man was all scrunched up

and trapped inside. Huge chains with large iron padlocks kept him inside. He looked like he hadn't bathed in weeks, and smelled awful.

"What's going on here?" Chris exclaimed. "You can't keep him like that!"

"This," Pastor Work calmly stated, "is not our work. It's his own doing. Just ask him."

Chris slowly approached the cage. "Hello?"

The man in the cage barely moved to look up. "What do you want?"

"Why are you in there?"

"I'm in here because I decided to get off the treadmill and live a normal life in the town of Everything Outside the Christian Religion. I was once a true believer of the faith, living in Christian Subculture, but I was enticed by the things of Everything Outside the Christian Religion and now I've been told I'm backslidden; I'm an unrepentant prodigal son. I've crucified Christ all over again (Hebrews 6:6), and there is no hope for me. I put myself in this cage as a symbol of my condition. There is nothing to be done for me. I can't save myself and God has turned his back on me. In fact, though I put myself in here, I know it was really God who did it. He's shut me out forever."

Chris looked at him. "Who told you that?"

"No one...er, well, everyone in Christian Subculture, really. But it's all true and right. I've seen it in the Book. They showed me. What they say about me is true."

Christian Books stepped forward. "Let this man be a warning to you, Chris. Use this image to your advantage to keep you on the treadmill, ever faster, never stopping, always focusing on the narrow beam, not looking right or left, and certainly not jumping off to journey left or right. You have one purpose from God, and one only. He knows what it is and though he didn't tell you, you must grind it out to find what it is and then do it with all your heart, soul and mind. This is the way to always keep God happy. But if you go to the right or the left, turning from the path God has for you, God will turn his back on you and things will go terribly wrong in your life. God will leave you behind, never to give you good things ever again. It's guaranteed. So let this be a horrible, terrifying and God-awful warning to you to live in submission, service and slavery to the God of love, mercy, and compassion every day of your life, every minute of your life, *every second of your life*. For eternity. That's what's required."

Chris realized from his discussions with Freedom that none of the parts of the Book the man in the cage mentioned actually meant what he thought they meant. He suddenly realized the man was in a self-imposed prison for no reason.

It was all such a waste.

Chris looked upon the man's situation with incredible pain and heartache. *What can be done for him? Somebody's got to do something...*

Luckily, Freedom had heard everything in Chris' earpiece and at that very moment was headed down the stairs behind them.

Freedom ignored everyone in the room and went straight to the man in the cage.

"Sir," Freedom addressed him. "I heard everything you said, and none of that is possible. Man cannot undo what God has done (2 Tim 2:13). None of those references to the Book you gave are correct. You've merely misinterpreted them. But it's not all your fault, no. Those things were probably taught to you by folks like Pastor Work, that fellow Sermons over there, and his side-kick Christian

Books. But they simply aren't true."

Freedom stood quiet for a moment, then waved his hand and all the locks and chains melted away. Not only that, but the iron cage itself disappeared into thin air. "This is what the Book says God has done for you," Freedom told him. "It's set in stone forever and nothing you can do can erase or reverse it."

With that, the man slowly stood upright and stretched his arms above his head. "Wow! That feels great! I'm out in the open air once again!"

"It gets even better when you come to the party," Chris told him excitedly.

The man looked at Freedom, as if looking for permission.

Freedom assured him, "Go in the peace and rest of God. And enjoy your life once more."

And Freedom, along with Chris and the formerly caged man, walked right past the other men and left the house of Questionable Interpretation.

As they walked across the yard, the last remaining bits of Chris' burden fell to the ground and dissolved away.

He was completely free. Free at last.

Chapter 18

The Pilgrim Rejoins The Party With New Friends

So Chris, Freedom and the man from the iron cage walked to the party.

On the way they passed several people.

They were named Simple, Sloth, Presumption, Formality, Hypocrisy, Fearful, Mistrust, and Danger. They said the most ridiculous things to our trio, who merely brushed off their words and invited them to the party.

Surprisingly, they all came.

The minute they arrived at the party the King ceremonially changed their names to Evolving, Wide Open Spaces, Endless Possibilities, Excitement, Contentment, Peace, Undetermined Future, and Fun.

* * *

In my dream, I saw a climbing wall at the party, and everyone enjoyed taking turns challenging themselves to make it to the top.

One man chastised himself heavily for resting halfway up, for he felt he was wasting the opportunity given him by the King to get to the top as quickly as possible. He was wearing a sweatshirt. On the sweatshirt was printed Ephesians 5:15-17.

The King looked up from a conversation across the room and called out, "There's no time limit. We'll be here awhile. Take your time."

The man pointed to his sweatshirt, "But musn't we always be going and doing as much as we can without stopping or hesitation?"

"No," the King replied. "The context of what's on your shirt (the point of the book of Ephesians) is Paul persuading two contentious groups to come together in unity and freedom. That's the only point of Ephesians."

"And they did that eventually, right?" Chris chimed in. "It was accomplished way back in history precisely because of those New Testament letters, correct?"

"Correct. Both sides have been unified long ago under Christ, thanks to the NT letters and the books of Ephesians and Romans in particular. All is well."

"But aren't the days evil?" the man quizzed.

"The days *were* evil, in the context Paul was writing. There was great persecution against those opting for freedom in those days, so if they didn't support each other in solidarity they would've had a much harder time. The freedom given by Christ would've been in great danger had those early men and women not held it together. Today, in the West, folks enjoy the fruits of their labor and, again, the fact that those letters were hugely instrumental in bringing us to where we are today."

"Excellent," Chris observed.

The man in the sweatshirt was greatly relieved. It was getting warm near the top, so he took off the sweatshirt and threw it down in a heap.

No one picked it up.

When the man came back down, another person began climbing the wall and she took so long the others in line were getting ancy.

The King called to her, "You look like you're having great difficulty."

"Yes," she said, "I fear there's only one way to climb this wall, and if I choose a wrong step I'll be sent back to the beginning, just as when the Hebrews wandered the wilderness for years on end because in their sin they didn't always choose the correct course."

"I assure you," the King assured her, "you have the freedom to choose any way you like, only know that some ways are more beneficial than others. There is not one prescribed way to adhere to, and if not, you suffer consequences. Haven't you heard? There's a new covenant now. The contract with the descendants of Isaac in the Old Testament has been fulfilled and it's finished. Now there's freedom. Besides, the old covenant was only between myself and the descendants of Isaac anyway. I notice you are not of that linage, so please relax."

The woman responded, "I have some of the rules from that contract written on the wall in my office. Ten of them, in fact. I'm a lawyer and I thought they applied to everyone. That's why they're on my wall. I'm being pressured to take them down, but I've been fighting it tooth and nail."

"Well, I'm happy to report that you're in the clear. You can take them down. They never applied to *anyone* after 33 AD, and only applied to a very specific lineage of people before that anyway. So it's all good. You can relax. Put up a poster of your favorite rock band in its place. Maybe Ozzy, Judas Priest, Metallica or Motely Crue. They're all excellent bands."

A man near the food table named Backward Masking nearly choked on a nacho. "You mean the

King likes rock music? Who would've thought?" And he pulled out his birth certificate and changed his name from Backward Masking to Really Good Music. He slapped an iPod in his ears and air-guitared for hours on end in a back corner of the party.

He badly wanted to make up for lost time.

Chapter 19

The Pilgrim Goes To Vanity Fair

As it was getting close to Christmas, Chris left the party momentarily to make a trip to a suburb of Everything Outside the Christian Religion called Vanity Fair.

Vanity Fair was not so much a suburb as it was the largest shopping mall in the world. The shopping mall filled the limits of the town. The mayor's office was squeezed between Spencer's Gifts and the Radio Shack.

There, in Vanity Fair, all manner of things were bought and sold.

All manner of things.

Chris neared an electronics store (not Radio Shack) because his wife loved gadgets of all kinds.

As he entered the store, a disheveled man approached him.

"Everything here is useless, worthless! A chasing after the wind," the man exclaimed.

Chris thought for a moment. "Well, my man, if I'm not mistaken, I think you're quoting from the book of Ecclesiastes, and again, if I'm not mistaken, context matters. The context of Ecclesiastes is the author trying to find meaning in life. And he concludes that meaning is not to be found in 'stuff.' It's just stuff. But stuff in and of itself is not intrinsically evil. What matters is the context of meaning in which it is placed. True, if you think material things are all there is to life, you will be left empty, for they don't have the power to sustain fulfillment. But with God, the creator who is infinitely creative, stuff can be, and is, fun and good in its proper context. Nothing wrong with that."

The man rubbed his chin. "I'm not so sure. I think it's *all* worthless and God will burn it all up one day. So don't bother with any of it. Get away while you can!"

Chris shook his head and went into the store. He found an awesome gadget he knew his wife would enjoy.

He was exiting the mall to return to the party when another wild-eyed man ran up to him.

"The world is full of temptations!" the man exclaimed. "We must be wary of the 'World'!"

Chris looked inquisitive. "Why, exactly, or what, do we need to be wary of?"

The man responded quick as the dickens. "You can be tempted just like Jesus was tempted by Satan! We can be sidetracked and enslaved by the wiles of the Devil..."

"Well," Chris responded. "I'm pretty sure I don't need to be sidetracked or tempted away from anything I'm doing in *my* life, because I am, in fact, not Jesus. I was just buying an electronic gadget for my wife."

"But isn't your goal to become Christlike, sonny? Isn't that what the Book tells us is the goal of life?"

"In a word: No. It's not. I don't need Satan to try and sidetrack me as happened with Jesus in the wilderness because I'm not on my way to eventually die on the cross for the sins of the world so humans can be reconciled to God. I'm pretty sure that's not me. It was *him*, I'm pretty sure, but it's not me. So I'm thinking that doesn't really apply to me. It applied to him, for sure. But not me. I think, once again, he did that so we can be free. I'm pretty sure that was the point (Galatians 5:1). I'm pretty sure I was made free for that very reason; so that I don't have to run around worrying about the devil tempting me, or worrying that the devil will derail my life. Anyway, as far as Satan offering Jesus the world, and saying angels would save him if he threw himself off the temple, I'm pretty sure none of that's me. I'm hardly in the position of Hitler or Napoleon or any of those guys who actually did try to take over the world. I don't even want to be president of the United States for Chrissakes. Screw that. Too much stress for me."

The man pressed forward. "Don't you lust for power? Doesn't everyone?"

"Well, if I did I'm sure the consequences would be far different than being in danger of Satan throwing me off a tower, or the edge of the temple, as it were. I don't think the fate of the salvation of all humanity would be in jeopardy. I think if I lusted for power the only consequences I would suffer would be that I'd have an unnecessary amount of constant discontentment in my life. In other words, I'd have a shitty life that would only harm me and those around me. Seems pretty simple. Don't really think there's some huge, cosmic drama being played out in the background or anything."

"So anyway, you say you're not really interested in becoming Christlike, huh?"

"Yeah, I don't even know what that means. What does it mean to be like Christ? Should I wear my hair like his? Should I berate teachers of the Law of Moses? Where do I even *find* teachers of the Law of Moses these days? But even if I could find them, I don't think I'd need to berate them like Jesus did. I think it's enough to know that Jesus fulfilled the Law and now we have no need of written codes in our dealings with God (Romans 7:6, book of Hebrews, especially chapter 10)."

"This is no laughing matter, sonny."

"I'm serious. Should I go find twelve people to be my disciples as I live out the Law of Moses perfectly and then die on a cross? Is that how I should be Christlike? Should I wash people's feet? I mean, we might actually be getting somewhere with that, since it is a good thing to love others. I think we can agree there."

"No! It's more than that! It's perfecting ourselves…"

"Well, ok. Good luck with that. I'm going back to the party to relax with my family and friends. I might not even wash anyone's feet, but I might offer them some of that awesome cheese dip. Have a good day, sir."

And Chris made his way back to the party.

Chapter 20

The Pilgrim, The King And Mr. Worldly-Wise Engage in Conversation

When Chris returned to the party, he gave his wife the Christmas gift. She enjoyed it very much, just as he knew she would.

He smiled and kissed her, then turned and got the shock of his life: He saw Mr. Worldly-Wise and Freedom holding a discussion with none other than the King himself!

He had to know what this was about, so he walked over.

Freedom was speaking: "An unfortunate effect of this is that it's killed creativity. If we live amidst a fixed backdrop, or grid, of predetermined history put in place by God at the beginning of time then all is said and done, right? All is determined. And this is how people have viewed the Book for centuries. And as I said, it's had the terrible effect of killing creativity."

Chris was surprised to find Mr. Worldly-Wise nodding in agreement, along with the King himself.

"Yes," the King nodded. "All that music and literature you have on you Worldly, most of it is very, very good. It's art and creativity at it's finest. I'm afraid a predetermined, background-grid view of history has indeed killed creativity in Christian

Subculture, frankly a place I rarely visit for that very reason."

Freedom nodded. "Yes, theologians have given the impression the Book is instructions for exactly how we are to live in the foreground of this fixed grid. But the Book actually says something different. Quite different."

The King chimed in, "When I set Adam and Eve loose in the Garden in Genesis 1 and 2, my intent was for them to be free to explore, create culture, create music, live, love and laugh without restraint. Well, they had only one restraint at that time. Just one. But now you all have *none*."

Chris was shocked.

The King saw this and turned to him. "That's right. None. Zero. Goose egg. I'm done with the sin and death part of history."

Freedom nodded. "Yes, as you can see from the party, the King now lives with humans permanently as he set us loose (one second after he rose from the dead) to create culture, music, literature, and to live, laugh and love *without* restraint. That's what the cross did. That's what freedom is. Paul says since this is true, do what's beneficial. Don't do what is harmful. It only makes sense. Do not destroy what God is rebuilding. That would be dumb. Go the direction God is going. You don't *have* to. But you have the opportunity to *want* to. Because that is what love is. It doesn't force or coerce. Ever."

The King nodded in agreement.

Chris offered to recap the discussion so far. "Let me see if I'm getting this right. So you're saying that an unfortunate side-effect of how the Book has been viewed in Christian Subculture is that a predetermined flow of history has killed creativity."

Freedom nodded. "Yes. Literature and music

and anything cultural, or *anything at all* for that matter, has been viewed by Christian subculture as only useful as a 'tool' to 'save' people; with no value in and of itself. And it's killed creativity. It's made people small. But what's the *actual* space we live in under the cross that gave freedom? It's wide open. Unexplored. Endless possibilities. Room for infinite human creativity. In *every* area of life. We don't worry on a minute-by-minute basis about how God views us. In fact, we don't worry *ever* how God views us. Because we know we are always, always, always, no matter what, 100 percent loved and accepted. We are *not* on treadmills of growth toward God or perfecting ourselves. We are not to be constantly stressing about God's plan for us, or what he wants us to do. What did he tell Adam and Eve? Be fruitful and multiply. Take care of the earth. Explore it. Discover it. Live in it and love it. And love life. Go nuts.

"That is what he told them. And that is what he tells us now. We can make bad decisions, yes, but God doesn't have to leave us. And he won't. That's the price he paid on the cross to gain for himself. That's how much he loves us. That's how much he wants to be *with us*. Always. He wants to be with us always."

Freedom looked at the King as if to say *I'm not trying to put words in your mouth...*

The King nodded. "You're doing pretty well. Keep going."

So Freedom did. "We've had a picture of theology where the game is about whether or not *we* want to be with God. Actually, the Book tells the story of a God who pursued humans in love to the very point of his own death—and now he can be with them forever. He doesn't have to destroy them because of their evil and the harm they do to those he loves. He doesn't have to withdraw from them because of their actions. He no longer has to worry that those things will separate him from humans. He can be with them always, because he paid the price of judgment for their evil. Isn't that incredible? And I don't say these things to get you to live lives of guilt and gratitude on your treadmills. No. What I just described is a truth. It's a fact. God saved us. Nothing is needed, or required, on our part. We just need to understand this if we want to live life more abundantly. The fact that I have blue eyes is a truth that doesn't require a response from me. My eyes are blue and that information is there no matter what I think or feel about it. That is what the Book is trying to communicate. That is what people have missed. That is why Jesus, Paul, and all the New Testament writers did not prescribe a formula for 'salvation' that requires your response. The NT writers were simply excited to tell the news about an event that *happened* and it *changed everything.* An event that changed the course of history, the course of creation, and most importantly, changed forever how humans relate to God, and vice-versa. Between humans and God, *ALL* has been finished. Both parties are at rest with each other. No more religion or rituals of any kind or superstitious nonsense whatsoever is required.

"None of it.

"Nada.

"Nothing.

"Zip.

"We're free.

"We live in the presence of a perfect God who loves us perfectly. And God will always be revealed to be better and better than we ever thought, because he's infinite.

"Always creating, always exciting. Never boxed in. Never constrained by us or what we think of him.

"He's wild, free and totally loving.

"And we can live that way with him.

"We are invited to.

"But we are not *forced* to.

"It's happening in our midst whether we like it or not, and whether we know it or not.

"It *is* happening.

"Creation *is* being healed and restored.

"That is the message of the Book.

"So to sum up: 2,000 years ago we were set free from any predetermined view of history. The only thing that is predetermined, or a given of history, is the fact that God's love reigns, not evil, sin, death or destruction.

"This is incredibly good news.

"It means that we can go back to the Garden of Eden and imagine what life was meant to be like. The first humans had freedom to do anything, except one thing. Today, after what Jesus did 2,000 years ago, we have freedom to do *anything*, without exception. There is not even *one* thing we can do to separate ourselves from God. Not *one* thing."

Chris sat back and thought about all that Freedom said. He marveled that the King was there and didn't stop him or disagree with any of it.

Even Mr. Worldly-Wise seemed to enjoy the discussion.

Chapter 21

The Pilgrim Meets The Harvester

Next I saw in my dream that a man named Harvester walked up to the party and threw down his tools. "I heard it's the end of work. Good! Because I'm done working. Forever. Let's party!"

"Actually, yes, welcome to the party, Harvester," Freedom greeted him. "But I think you might've misunderstood something. This isn't about not *physically* working. We still must cultivate the land and have jobs so society will function properly."

"How about just not working so hard?"

"Well, no, it's not about working less hard either. It's about your spiritual life. How you view your relationship to God. There's nothing wrong with working—and working hard—at your physical work. That's a good thing, actually. An ethic of working hard is a *great* thing. We're talking about rest in your soul and spirit. We're talking about realizing you don't have to do anything—work—to keep God happy and to stay on his good side. There is nothing we need to do for God. He has everything and he is fine. And we don't work for him out of gratitude for what he did on the cross, either. Yes, we were bought with a price, but he doesn't ask to be paid back. In fact, we *can't* pay him back. And we don't need to grovel about that, either. God is happy that this was done for us, and now is the time to rest and celebrate in our relationships with God."

The King stepped forward. "Yes, yes, very good. That is true, Freedom. People were made to move forward, to create, to produce. There's nothing wrong with that. It's the compartmentalization that's the problem. Religious life vs. secular life. Sacred space vs. the profane.

"Yes," Freedom piped in, "after Jesus, these things were not meant to be separate. All space is space. All life is life. We live our lives in space and in freedom. We get an education, we work jobs, we have families and we love people. It's that simple. Do what is beneficial, don't do what is harmful. Paul says this in 1 Corinthians 6:12 and 10:23. It's that simple.

"Jesus bridged the gap and canceled the sin barrier so God can be with people. God went to the cross to show what love is, and so that he could be with people. Folks in the largely 'Christian' Western hemisphere have made salvation a personal, individual thing—the cross gets us into heaven. And yes, that's part of it, but it's not the main point.

"The main story in the Book is that God wants to be with people, but the existence of sin caused a gulf—a barrier—to a free flowing relationship because evil must be judged. So God provided a solution to that—for us and *himself*."

The King stepped in: "And because 2,000 years ago Jesus set in motion the reversal of the effects of sin, where are we heading now?"

"Good question," said Harvester.

Freedom continued, "Well, Jesus took us back to the Garden. The garden started with two people who lived in a physical world without sin. Sin entered, and it caused a rift between people and God. God had to judge people who hurt other people (whom he loved). This is only natural, and the same thing we would do when we defend our own loved ones against wrong-doing. So now that Jesus patched everything up, and took away the sin of the world, we're on our way to reversing the effects of sin and evil in the world. The effects of sin are slowly being erased from the collective human race. So is death. That is the great news of the Book. And one day in the future, as we see in Revelation chapters 21 and 22, sin and death will be non-factors for humans. It will be gone from earth entirely. Free-will is not eradicated, but no one who continues to participate in evil can live in the city described in Revelation 21 and 22. Humans will then live as God originally intended in the Garden, only now, it's a city, because there are a lot more people.

"Do this exercise: Read Genesis 1 and 2 (note there is loneliness, work and the free-will ability to choose against God in the Garden. These things are not sin, or a result of sin), and then go straight to reading Revelation 21 and 22. That was God's original intention for mankind. Sin was a side note, a sidetrack. It was a problem, God took care of it 2,000 years ago, and now we're back on track.

"Next, imagine this: We can get a sense for what God intends for us now if we merely imagine what the Garden of Eden, and an eventually populated earth, would've looked like had sin never entered the picture.

"What would life have been like? They would have gone to Disneyland, built space shuttles, gotten educations at Harvard and Oxford, explored evolution and DNA and would've been taken to the hospital after they fell out of trees..."

"Wait, wait, wait...hospital? In paradise?" Harvester asked.

"Yes, gravity is a natural law of physics. It

wasn't something invented after the fall or because of evil. If Adam climbed a tree and fell, he would've broken his arm and went to the hospital—well, after he and Eve popped out some kids who became doctors."

"Doctors?"

"Yes, again, doctors deal with more than just results of 'The Fall' (disease and such). They also deal with the effects of gravity."

"But why wouldn't God instantly heal them? Or have angels catch them if they fell out of trees?"

"Is that the picture we get from Genesis 1 and 2? That God created people and the world with built-in pain and healing systems so he could *coddle* them? Or did he make the world the way it is, with pain and healing built in so that people would live normally in a natural world—to cultivate it, explore it and thrive in it? I think we make the mistake of thinking that pain itself was a result of 'The Fall.' That any and all pain is of the devil and God would wipe it out if he could. But think about this for a moment: Why would God create our bodies with the incredible capacity to heal itself? Was this placed in humans *after* the fall? No, pain is a good thing that lets the person know something has gone wrong and needs attention. It's not evil, or a result of The Fall. Pain, as I imagine God originally intended it, shows us where the boundaries are. Imagine this: Who is better prepared for this world? A child who occasionally smacks herself around on the playground, getting cuts and scrapes, and thus learns the limits of what she can and can't do at an early age when she is most resilient, or a child who is never allowed to experience the consequences of their actions? Which one is learning the limits of the natural world?"

Chris looked puzzled. "But wouldn't that be like the movie Groundhog Day where the main character can always hurt himself to the point of death, but he never dies, so he just becomes callous like he's superhuman?"

"But if death is not in the picture, then what would be the point of needing to feel 'superhuman?' In a world without death, it's not profitable to move yourself in the direction of intentionally hurting yourself. There would be better things to do. Such as hiking, exploring nature, enjoying a sunrise or sunset, building rockets and exploring the universe. Some people say they wouldn't want to live forever, but that's because we tire of things on earth because our bodies wear out, we get emotionally and physically drained over our lifetimes from the effects of evil and sin. These are not good things. But interestingly, as humans we automatically assume life after death. All of us do. It is actually incredibly difficult to imagine that after being alive and existing, we would then revert to a state of eternal non-existence. That is *hard* to believe. Many people say they believe this, but nobody lives like they believe it. Everyone lives as if things have meaning. And deep meaning. Not just meaning artificially assigned to it for the moment (existentialism). Deep down, we seem to *know* that life goes on *somehow* after death, and that eternal non-consciousness is actually very difficult to conceive of. Let me ask you: Which seems more natural to us? Eternal life, or eternal non-consciousness?"

Chris was thinking hard, "Ok, I follow you, but I'm still wondering about falling from trees and breaking arms and such. If any kid fell from a tree, they'd probably cry. Doesn't Revelation say that 'in the end every tear will be wiped away.' What about that?"

"Yes, and let's look at the context of that book. The book of Revelation was written to encourage those who were under the horrible persecution in Rome, especially during Nero, and many other places around the near East at that time. I'm sure we can safely say there was an incredible amount of sorrow (tears) from families whose husbands, wives, children and parents were dragged off and imprisoned, tortured and/or killed. When John talks of every tear being dried, I believe he was speaking of the effects of evil. Not the effects of natural laws. God built a world with the possibility that humans could get hurt (and amazingly their bodies would heal) *before* Genesis 3. Evil was not in it. Later, in Genesis 3, evil was introduced by mankind."

"But don't we experience injury only because of evil?"

"No, not necessarily. If you climb a tree and slip, fall and break your arm, is evil involved? No, it's just a natural process. Adam and Eve would've put their arms in a sling, felt pain for awhile, then went on with life after it healed. As to angels saving them every time they were going to hurt themselves, I think, again, God would not have made our bodies capable of pain (a *good* alert system) and healing itself. There'd be no need."

"But isn't a lot of pain to our bodies because of the degeneration of our bodies toward death? What about that?"

"According to human biologists, the body's capacity to heal itself is more resilient than we think. It's actually quite surprising to physiologists that the body degenerates and dies at all. Death is the *unreasonable* occurrence. Physiologists have a very difficult time explaining why the body dies in light of the body's incredible capacity to sustain itself. In other words, when it comes to our bodies, death seems to be an anomaly, not the given."

The King chimed in again, "So, yes, in terms of life now, we can imagine that life would be exactly the same, only without evil present."

Chris questioned, "But the effects of evil are still present *now*, even though Jesus conquered death and sin."

"True."

"So why not wipe it out the moment Jesus rose from the dead?"

"Because of free-will. People are not robots. Adam and Eve had the ability to choose evil even before 'The Fall,' but at that time, evil didn't reign. Since Jesus, evil no longer reigns, but people still have choice. What is happening in history now is the slow eradication of the effects of evil from the world as things are worked out. I admit, it's all a bit hard for the finite mind to grasp, but think of it like this: The more and more you pour clear water into water thick with blue food-coloring, the more and more clear water dominates, to the point where eventually you won't see any blue at all. And the clear water represents love. God's love, and the love of people for each other. It's kind of like that. Paul says by renewing our minds, by thinking of things differently, we can do what is beneficial and not do what is harmful.

"On a societal level, this means we can make laws for society that are appropriate for the time period in which we live. These laws can change over time. That is ok. There are no longer any 'written codes' set in stone (literally or figuratively). What is appropriate now may not apply years from now. We can figure this out. God lives with us as a helper. It's not rocket science."

"God actually trusts humans—evil, fallen humans—to do this?" Harvester asked.

"Yes, God is amazingly optimistic when it comes to humans, even if we aren't. God is moving in a direction: The direction of love, healing and the restoration of all things. We can agree with that, or go against it. If we go against the grain, we will not find life. Only death and destruction, and God does not support that, and will not be found there. Eventually, things will be as they are described in Revelation 21 and 22. Jesus set this in motion 2,000 years ago with the full force of God's love, and nothing will stop God's love. Humans still have free will and their choices still matter, but overall, God's love reigns, not evil. And God's love will reign more and more and more as time goes on. That is the picture we get from the Book."

Chapter 22

The Pilgrim Watches The King Free More People

Then in my dream I saw there were some people hanging out in a corner of the party.

About twenty-five people.

They had looks of great distress on their faces and were praying fervently, their cheeks flowing with tears.

"What are they doing?" Chris asked Freedom.

"Oh, that group calls themselves 2 Chronicles 7:14. They believe their country is degenerating quickly into moral decadence and God will judge them harshly for it, or has already, by sending natural disasters, diseases and terrorist strikes to their country. They believe that if the people of God 'repent,' God will hear them and heal their land. The verse they like to quote from the Book is, 'If my people should turn from their ways and repent, I will hear them and heal their land.'"

"Huh," Chris thought. "That's interesting. So what to do? By the looks of it, seems like a terrible way to live."

"It is," the King said, stepping over to the group. "So maybe I can help."

Everyone in the group stopped straining, crying and praying to look up for a moment.

"Here's the deal guys," the King started, "that verse is about a specific group of people (the descendants of Isaac) at a specific point in time (the Old Testament) who were under a specific contract between themselves and me, called the Mosaic Law. The terms of the Law contract went like this: "If you follow me and do what I say, I will bless you. If not, I will curse you" (Deut. 28). The intention of this was not to enslave people into doing it, but, in fact, to show that humans *can't* do it. I never thought they could do it. All I wanted them to do is recognize that they couldn't. I simply wanted them to understand there is a gulf—a separation—between them and me; a problem in need of a solution (Galatians 3:24). Eventually, the whole thing would be solved by Jesus on the cross, but until then, all I wanted was for them to stop being so bullheaded and come to me with a humble spirit (Psalm 51:17), and admit they couldn't live up to the impossibly high standard of The Law; how to treat people perfectly. The standard was perfection. That is my character. I love everyone perfectly, all the time. And it's pretty cool. But I digress a bit. Back to my point: So I told them— those specific people in the Old Testament who were in this specific contract with me—that if they simply came to me, and admitted they were failing at loving those around them, I would curtail, or relent, the terms of the contract between us and not curse them, but heal them instead. Simple as that.

"Problem was, most times they were too prideful and stuck enjoying their ways of evil to come to me. They enjoyed hurting others, and were so calloused to evil they didn't even care how much it would cost them personally (Isaiah, Ezekiel and Jeremiah). I had to stand up for the victims and stop the evil. That's how much I love people, especially the victims of evil.

"All that stuff was recorded in the Book as an object lesson for the whole world to see. It reveals the utter destructiveness of the human heart run amok.

"Anyway, since you can clearly see that none of that applies to the relationship between you and I today (and never applied to you Gentiles anyway), you can all get up and join the party. You're free. A new contract is in place, a new agreement. This agreement says that I've taken care of everything, so now there's no outstanding business between us (Hebrews).

"It's all been finished.

"We are on good terms and always will be. So you all can get up and join the party and celebrate with everyone."

And since he was the King, everyone believed him. The people in the corner wiped away their tears, put smiles on their faces and ran to the party as fast as they could.

They were greatly relieved at the words of the King.

Chapter 23

The Pilgrim Gets His Name Changed

When it got late, though the party was in no way winding down or slacking in intensity of joy and celebration, Chris nonetheless found himself tired.

He was merely worn out from the day.

Since his house was a good piece away, Freedom offered to let him stay at his home on the edge of the festivities.

Chris accepted the gracious invitation.

Once inside the house the two sat at the kitchen table.

"I'll put some coffee on and we can chat," Freedom offered.

Chris liked the idea and accepted the gracious hospitality.

Freedom put two steaming cups before them and asked, "So your name is Chris, but you haven't told me your full name yet. What is it?"

"My full name is Judaia Christian Muslim Smith."

Freedom looked surprised. "And that's on your birth certificate?"

"Well, yes. My parents wanted to name me after the three great monotheistic religions of the world. I think it's pretty cool."

"Yes, but is it accurate?"

"Sure. It's my name. It's on my birth

certificate."

"No, I wasn't talking about that."

"What do you mean?"

"Are those really the three great monotheistic religions of the world? Judaism, Christianity and Islam?"

"Well, yes. Why not? Everyone knows it. It's not disputed."

"In a sense, yes, it's what everyone thinks. But let's unpack it in light of what you've learned lately."

"Ok."

"First, I would view a religion as being something where there is still unfinished work to be done by humans vis-à-vis their relation to God. Something you *follow*. In other words, for Jews, the OT law and rituals are to be followed, and if not, God is not happy. In Islam, the five pillars of Islam are to be followed or God is unhappy.

"But Christianity? Well, sadly, since what is written in the Book *has* been turned into a religion, people still think there are rules and rituals and things to be done to appease God, even if they are living under a system of 'grace.' The way people live out Christianity is actually no different in practice than Judaism and Islam. People live as if things are still 'unfinished' (the treadmill of 'sanctification' being the biggest offender). But I think, as you've seen through events and our discussions of late, that what is thought of as 'Christianity' is really not what the Book is trying to communicate at all. The Book is *not* offering a choice among other choices that one might select out of the buffet of religious or philosophical ideas. We do not get 'saved' and then work to follow the Book carefully our whole lives as we 'work out our salvation with fear and trembling'— another oft misunderstood verse.

"Working out our salvation with fear and trembling means that we understand fully that God did something in history 2,000 years ago that set the world on a different path, and everything changed. Not that we work to change ourselves to conform to what God is doing, but that he simply *did* something and it changed everything about the way we relate to him. He started the enormous project of healing and restoring all of creation and we live in the middle of that—we're *all* in the middle of that. We're all in the middle of God healing and restoring creation to what he intended before sin entered the world. So the Book isn't communicating a system to be individually and minutely lived. Nor is it a system of morality, or a system of rules and rituals mandated by God to keep him happy. No. It's *freedom*. We were set free by God so that he never has to be unhappy or displeased with us.

"The Book is not the story of the human race. It's the autobiography of God. God is the point. History is about the good things God did, the good things God is doing, and the good God will continue to do. And we're all in on it. We can enjoy the ride. This doesn't mean life will always be easy or comfortable. But it does mean God will always be with us and for us—with all authority and power—and God will never leave us. God is always committed to our good, no matter what. We live in freedom."

Chris leaned in. "Hmm. That's good. I like it. So what you're saying is that the Book doesn't so much present an ongoing systematic way to live life with God—which is religion—but it's actually a one-time truth that happened in history (the cross) that changed everything. Now we simply live free in the knowledge that God is healing and restoring everything with his power, his energy and his plans...something like that?"

"Yes, exactly."

"So are we passive in this? Is that what freedom means? That we do nothing?"

"No, freedom means we're off the hook. What God does or doesn't do in relation to us is no longer dependant on us. In other words, we can participate with him in the healing and restoring of the world in his energy, power and plans by resting in our souls. And if we don't want to participate, we are free not to. We *can* simply live our lives. But those who practice intentional evil—the harming of others continually and intentionally—are not moving in the direction God is. There is no place in God's kingdom for that. And God will deal with it however he chooses. We can trust him in that. He probably won't deal with it with eternal Hell as is commonly taught, but somehow, in his wisdom and knowledge, we can trust that he'll deal with it.

"And when we talk about a continual practice of evil, we're not talking about gossiping a few times at work, or cutting someone off in traffic or smoking in the boy's room—those sorts of things. It's not that."

"But doesn't James 2:10 state guilty of breaking one law makes us guilty of the whole law?"

"Well, that is quoted a lot as being the basis for the theological idea of one sin and you're culpable before God for breaking all his laws. But we need to rethink that since James was addressing those who were trying to live under the 613 Laws of Moses instead of 'under the law that gives freedom' (James 1:25, 2:12; Galatians 5:1).

"So under the Law of Moses—it was true: Guilty of one law, guilty of the whole law. But

Gentiles aren't, and never were, under the Mosaic Law. In Romans, Paul says Gentiles' consciences acted as the Law to them. Therefore, Paul states *all* sinned and fall short of the glory of God. But then God solved the sin problem for Jews and Gentiles alike by taking away the sin of the world. For all time and forever, as far as the East is from the West. *No human* now lives under a contractual agreement with God. We don't sign on the dotted line for salvation and if not, we're out. It is much more gracious, mysterious and merciful than that."

"So universalism then?" Chris asked. "God accepts everyone and our decision and actions mean nothing? Freewill was effectively snuffed out by the cross?"

"No, it's not that either. It's just that things are a lot less 1+1 always has to equal 2 when it comes to humans in relation to God. How God deals with evil, or someone who wants to continue to destroy what he's trying to heal and restore, is not concretely clear. We don't know exactly. But do know we can leave it in God's hands to deal with in the best way possible. We don't have to sweat it.

"In society, we can, and must, still have a justice system. It's massively imperfect, but it's the best we have for now. However, the Book promises things can, and will, get better. In our personal lives we don't have to repay evil with evil. Nothing change in our relationships to God if we do. He will always be for and with us. But forgiveness is where life is found. Loving our enemies instead of destroying them will always be where life, and more life, is found. Love always wins. Love is always the best course. Where love is, God will always be found there."

"That's good stuff. A lot to think about," Chris

remarked.

"And that brings us to your name."

"Yeah, my name. I think it's in need of a change. Something that reflects less religion and more freedom. What should it be?"

"That's just it. Anything you like. You're free to choose."

"I've always liked 'Fred.' How about that?"

"Fred it is. From now on, you'll be Fred."

With that, they each took a last sip of coffee and turned in for the night.

Luckily, they were drinking decaf.

Chapter 24

The Pilgrim Has A Most Unfortunate Encounter

Fred woke early in the morning and decided to take a walk.

It turns out Freedom lived in a small village.

Fred walked past a coffee house with a bakery called "Church's Coffee and Donuts."

It smelled delicious!

Fred couldn't help himself. The aroma seemed so comforting and hospitable. It reminded him of home.

So he went in.

Fred was greeted by three hostesses who sat him at a nice table in the corner where the sun shone warmly through the window at just the right angle.

Warm, but not glaring.

Fred instantly felt refreshed; mentally and physically.

The hostesses served him coffee with a cheese Danish, then things took an odd turn.

Fred expected the coffee shop to be a place of comfort and support, but the nametags on the hostesses read: Unloving, Guilt, and Out of Context.

In a way, Fred was trapped in the nice atmosphere. The women had odd names, yes, but they seemed harmless enough.

So he decided to stay and enjoy his coffee and Danish.

His hostesses sat with him and asked, "Tell us about your journey so far."

"Well," he told them, "I haven't really been on a journey. I'm actually just living life. But for the longest time in my life I was hugely burdened by what I now recognize as trying to live the Book as the religion called 'Christianity.' Christian theology goes like this: People are 'saved' then they try and improve themselves daily so that one day they'll become like Christ. They call it being 'Christlike,' a process of sanctification. To do this, you get on a treadmill with a balance beam out in front and you concentrate on the narrowness of the beam, the narrowness of the path you're on, and don't—under any circumstances—go to the right or left. You can't even look those ways. It's dangerous. Or so I thought."

"Well, that sounds about right. We don't see any problems with that," Unloving said.

Fred ignored the comment. "But then this guy named Freedom came along and explained that the intent of the Book is not to prescribe a way of living day by day, hour by hour, minute by minute, but the Book actually communicates the news that something happened in history 2,000 years ago that changed the world. So the Book is not so much a 'religion' to be lived day in and day out with religious effort, but simply understanding a reality based upon an event that took place 2,000 years ago, namely, that God started a process of healing and restoring creation to the way he originally intended it in Genesis chapter 1 and 2."

"Yes," Guilt butted-in, "but this 'healing and

restoration' happens by us putting effort into making ourselves better; making ourselves more Christlike. That is how God intends for it to happen. Do you really think we can put in *no effort at all* and see things change?"

"Well, that's just it. We're commanded by Jesus to rest. And in Galatians 3:3 Paul tells us any transforming or restoration or healing comes from *God's* power, energy and plans, not *ours.* We participate in it by the power and energy and plans of God as we rest in our souls."

"Isn't that the same thing as putting no energy into it at all?"

"No, not really. Because if I'm resting, then I'm not worried, or striving, or stressed out, or living in fear of consequences of anything between me and God. I don't have to live 'outside my comfort zone' to do things for God. I don't have to serve people 24 hours a day, or supposedly worship God constantly, or read my Book *all the time,* or pray all the time, etc, etc. There is nothing I *have* to do for God or suffer consequences. It's none of that. I don't have to feel guilty all the time for not doing enough, or not following Jesus enough, or falling short of moral standards, or so-called failing God..."

"Not feel guilty!" Guilt shrieked. "But what will propel you to do what God wants you to do? What's the motivation?"

"That's just it. God doesn't *want or need* me to do *anything.* I *can* do things, but I don't *have* to, or else suffer consequences. That's the difference."

"But if you and I don't humanly do things, how will anything get done?" Guilt asked.

"God will do it, either way."

"But don't you see that makes no sense?"

"Then you don't know the God I know. Because

the God I know rarely makes sense."

"So where's your family?" Out of Context asked. "Are you married? Do you have children?"

"Yes."

"Well, it's important for you and for them that we get you straightened out and back on your treadmill. That's where God wants you to be."

"Definitely!" Guilt agreed. "You should be ashamed of yourself for thinking otherwise."

Fred shrunk back a bit at the forcefulness of Guilt. She damn near made him question everything Freedom had told him.

"Well, I...er..."

"No matter," Out of Context interjected. "We'll have you back on track in no time. So, have you been making sure your family comes with you on your journey?"

Fred looked at her blankly.

"You haven't, have you?" Guilt said flatly.

"Uh, what journey?" Fred stammered. "Freedom said life was about rest and..."

"No, that's silly-talk," Out of Context said. "The book of Ephesians tells us not to engage in silly-talk or coarse-jesting. Modern cuss-words are on the top of that list of course, but that's obvious and goes without saying..."

"You do love your family, don't you?" Guilt piped-in.

"Er, ah, yes, I mean, no," Fred caught himself. "Er, yes, yes I do! Very much. That's why I left them back at the party...I just went for a walk with Freedom to discuss some things, then..."

Guilt exploded. "You horrible man! You left your family at a *party*? Don't you know those things promote all kinds of debauchery and evil? *Sinners* are to be found at parties (Matthew 9:10-11;

Matthew 11:18-19)!"

"Well, I, ah..."

"No, no, no!" Unloving agreed. "You must not lead them to parties, or to such places where they can enjoy life. You need to save them! Your priority should be to make sure your family doesn't fall into destruction, into the eternal pit of Hell! You need to make sure this same thing for everyone around you. Everyone you meet, everyone in the whole world, in fact. Their eternal destinies either in heavenly bliss or in the lake of damndable fire depends solely on your actions. If your behavior is bad—sinning and immoral—they will be drawn away from God only to end up in eternal deathfire and hell-destruction. But if you are good, righteous and morally upright, they might see God and want to choose the way of eternal bliss with you and God."

The three women nodded their heads in agreement.

Then Guilt wagged a disappointed finger at him. "But if you are *bad*, they will all *most certainly* end up in Hell, and God will hold you responsible for it. Ezekiel 3:19 is clear on that point. However, if you are good they might decide they want to be with God....*but*, that's still no guarantee that they will...either way, if you were good, you have absolved yourself from responsibility and no longer have to feel sympathy for them as they get burned and tortured eternally in the lake of damndable-hellfire as you go on to eternal bliss."

"Huh?" Fred was confused. "What? My family? *I'm* going to be held responsible or absolved of responsibility for them going to Hell or not....by my *actions*? By whether I'm moral or immoral? By my *behavior*? And *that* will determine if they choose heaven or Hell for their eternity?"

"That's what it says in Ezekiel 3."

Fred was massively confused. It didn't seem logical, or even remotely loving, at any level.

And it gave a horrible picture of God.

"You do still do wrong things, correct?" Guilt asked.

"Well...yes. I can't deny that."

"We all do. That's why we need to make ourselves more like Christ. The eternal destinies of those around us depend on this. As an added bonus, we want to be cleansed of anything harmful in our hearts, right? If it was up to me, I'd never have to struggle with my friend Guilt here on anything ever again. But Romans 7 tells me that when I want to do good, evil is always right there with me disabling me from doing what I want to do. This constant struggle and internal conflict is simply part of our lives with God. It's just something we must struggle out."

At that moment, more confused than ever, Fred remembered the earplug in his pocket. He hoped Freedom was awake and listening on the other end.

He put the earplug in and it crackled to life. *"Hey, buddy. First let's cover that Ezekiel 3 thing. That's easy enough. As her name suggests, Out of Context totally took this one out of context. The beginning of Ezekiel 3 clearly sets this up as being a matter between God and the descendants of Isaac— and them only. They are the only ones under the Deut. 28 contract with God, which has nothing to do with us today, and never applied to Gentiles at any point in history anyway.*

"Second, and this one is a bit more tricky—not because it's any less obvious, but because everyone has had this quite wrong for centuries—and that is the matter of Romans 7. It's assumed that Romans chapter 7 is Paul discussing his struggle against 'sin'

in the context of his life as a 'believer' in Christ—-but he's not. In the overall context of this section of Romans, Paul is contrasting what choosing a life of freedom in Christ looks like compared with those of Jewish lineage wanting to continue living life under the Law. So Romans 7 is actually a picture of someone who would choose to continue living life under the Mosaic Law, as opposed to living in the freedom Jesus gave them (Romans 7:6, Galatians 5:1). And again, this choice is something that never applied to Gentiles anyway. In Romans 8, Paul says the best way for everyone *is to simply live with the Spirit of Christ in the wide open space of the freedom Christ gave you. There is no more need for anyone to live shackled under Law (written code) of any kind anymore."*

"Ok, good answers," Fred said quietly.

"What?" Unloving asked.

"Oh, nothing," Fred answered. "Well, once again, this has been swell but I'll be going now. It was nice to meet y.....er, well, it was nice to live for several minutes in the presence of you each of you...er, well, what the hell....it was really horrible to meet you all, and I didn't enjoy myself in the least. You are twice the daughters of Hell and not helpful to anyone. I find that appalling."

Everyone was stunned.

Fred looked around nervously. "So, anywho, without further ado, I'll be heading back to the celebration once again. Any of you want to join me?"

"Oh, hell no!" Unloving screeched as Guilt shot her a look. "I wouldn't be caught dead there."

"That's right," Fred said, nodding his head and chuckling. "You wouldn't."

He left the coffee shop vowing never to return to that awful place again.

Chapter 25

The Pilgrim Returns To The Party

I saw in my dream that as Fred left the coffee shop, a man came running up behind him.

"Hey, uh, the girls back there were worried about you, so they thought it best if I went with you on your journey."

"Oh, well, thanks, but there's no journey. I'm not on a journey. I'm just going back to the party."

"No, no. I insist. I'll be most helpful."

"I think I'll be all right by mysel..."

"No, I'll go with you. I'll be helpful. You'll see."

"Well," Fred looked worn out. "Ok, it might be a good thing. Come along then. What's your name?"

"My name's Self-Righteous, but some call me Anal."

"That doesn't sound good at all. Not sure you'll be of much help."

"Oh no, you'll see. We'll do this thing together. It'll be great!"

No sooner had they shook hands than an evil demon from Hell swooped down on the road and shot flaming arrows straight at them (Ephesians 6:16).

"Duck!" Fred yelled.

But there wasn't time.

Curiously, the arrows went right through them with no effect.

"Huh." Fred shrugged.

The demon was livid. "Why didn't anything happen? Why didn't you guys put up your shields of faith and gird your loins and shod your feet with the shoes of righteousness, and all that crap from Ephesians 6? I love it when you guys get all panty-bunched about that chapter. It's so entertaining."

At that moment, Freedom walked up.

"He has a point," Fred said, taking the side of the demon. "Aren't we involved in a colossal spiritual war? Us and angels and demons and all that, duking it out to the finish? Don't we need to be prepared?"

"In a word," Freedom replied, "no." Then he quoted, "'Greater is he who is in you than he who in the world.'"

The demon looked crest-fallen.

Freedom continued. "People in cultures of the first century dealt with the very real presence of evil spirits that were active in controlling their lives and cultures. We see this clearly from the demon possessions Jesus dealt with. These people had no say, and no power, in stopping demons who randomly possessed them and made life hell. It wasn't just mental illness. It was very real, very dark spiritual activity. And this horrendous debilitating fear of the dark, evil spirit world was one reason these people asked Jesus to 'save' them, and one of the main reasons Jesus brought the kingdom of God to earth. What the kingdom of God coming to earth meant to these people was that the power of the dark sprit world was broken. They no longer had to live in fear of it. The West is cynical about this today, thinking these people were simply 'backward,' or Stone-Age or superstitious for no reason. But that's because it's a non-factor for Western cultures today thanks to what Christ did. However, it's interesting to note that in some areas of the world today, dark spiritual activity still exists; the influence of the evil sprit world can still be felt and experienced in a very real, above-ground way in some places.

"So in summation, John and Peter and the New Testament writers were ecstatic to report that the power of the demon world was broken. The power and influence of Satan's kingdom was made null and void by the cross and there was no longer any reason to live in fear of it. This was incredibly good news to the people of that time in a way we can't even conceive of today, as the dark spirit world—at least in the West as we said—has all but been nullified."

Fred was incredulous. "So there's not a cosmic power-showdown behind the scenes for people's souls?"

"No, it's all been defeated. Any 'showdown' for souls, if there even is one, has nothing to do with the influence of Satan. He was defeated entirely by the cross."

Self-Righteous piped-in, "But what about Ephesians 6?"

"Good question. And it has a good answer. First, we must understand that the book of Ephesians is about one thing, and one thing only: Paul's attempt, and goal, to see Jews and Gentiles living *together* in love and peace under the freedom Christ gave them. Everything in Ephesians relates to this theme of trying to get them to get along under the umbrella of what Christ did on the cross in setting them free. Woven throughout the book of Ephesians is the theme of being submissive to each other out of respect. Paul uses examples such as marriage, children vis-à-vis their parents, as well as the tight relationship Jesus has with his bride, the church; the honor and respect between them. Paul uses everything he can think of to convince the Ephesians to live in unity—not in arrogance—toward each other. That is the way they should go forward, Paul says. And this *has* been accomplished in history precisely because of these letters of Paul.

"Ephesians 6 is the conclusion of Paul's argument for unity. He encourages them to know the truth, to reflect on salvation—that Jesus set everyone free. That God doesn't show favoritism, and there is neither slave (uneducated impoverished underclass) nor Greek (intellectual, financial elite), Jew nor Gentile, etc., as stated in Galatians. All things about Christ point to them laying aside their arrogance and feelings of favoritism before God to simply get along with each other in love. That is the point of the whole book. We, today, do *not* have an enormous Jew/Gentile split in our culture, so we can celebrate and be happy Paul cleared up a serious problem that was very real long ago."

"So should we never read the book of Ephesians ever again? Why bother?"

"There is tremendous merit in knowing these things, because it's a reflection of the power of God; the evidence that God *did* start a powerful work of healing and restoration (as Paul promised to the Philippians in Phil. 1:6) and it continues to this day even in our cultural and globalized context. So we are *not* trying to religiously live the words of Paul in Ephesians, or other books of the New Testament. We *are* to understand the overall context of the Biblical story and live in that reality, the reality that 2,000 years ago God started a process of healing and restoration of all things that continues to this day. Simple as that."

"I like that," Fred said.

Self-Righteous had a thought. "I might have to

change my name after hearing all this. Can you tell us more?"

Freedom smiled. "Gladly. So we see that contrary to popular belief, the Book is not a minutia of rules to live by. It is not a moral code of behavior to keep us in good standing with God. It is nowhere close to that. It *is* the simple announcement that God started something 2,000 years ago that continues to this day. And we celebrate the excitement of living in the midst of this renewal process, as we have the privilege to participate in it with no consequences between us and God if we choose to do a lot, or a little, or nothing at all. Jesus did not go to the cross to force us to follow God. God will *always* be with us and for us, no matter what. God is not a tyrant, and he deals with evil in his wisdom according to his love for the creation he is healing and restoring."

The demon piped in: "But what about the verse that states 'the devil is a prowling lion seeking someone to devour' (1 Peter 5:8)?"

Freedom nodded. "Hmm, yes. That verse is talking about those who in their freedom choose to practice a lifestyle of evil. And again, by 'evil,' we aren't talking about smoking in the boy's room or cutting someone off in traffic. This is about aligning yourselves with evil, in your actions and identity. There is still no condemnation from God, but it is a harmful and useless way to live, as Paul, John, Peter and Jude state in their letters. A person, or people, who chooses the continual practice of evil is devoured. They will not find life there. Only death, destruction and lies are in store. God will not be found there."

Self-Righteous gave a quizzical look. "So how is evil ultimately 'judged?'"

Freedom answered, "We don't know for sure. It's up to God. We can leave it with him and trust he knows best. Paul, Peter, John and Jude attempted to persuade folks with their letters to go the other way—in your freedom, live your identity as a child of God by living in love. Because that is where God and life are found. This is the way to the best life possible. For you and for everyone. Not by religiously living this identity, but by living as a child of God in rest."

Self-Righteous perked up. "That's it! I think I'll change my name to Child of God."

Freedom smiled. "Good choice."

As they made their way back to the party, the demon flew away saddened he didn't get to shoot anyone.

Conclusion

I hope you've enjoyed this retelling of *The Pilgrim's Progress*.

I hope it challenged you to think, and possibly reevaluate, some long staid theological notions.

God has given us freedom; the freedom to chart a course for ourselves with him alongside. He is less a cosmic policeman and more a cheerleader as we chart our destiny as the human race.

This world can get better.

Things *will* get better.

That is the promise of Revelation 21 and 22.

But *exactly* where things go, well, that's up to us.

We have freewill. And God is with us.

In Genesis 1 and 2, God put within Adam and Eve all the creative power and intelligence they needed to create a world that was exciting and full of challenge and discovery.

We still have that power in us. And we have the opportunity and responsibility to use it wisely.

Sin and death have been defeated.

There is no outstanding work to be done between us and God.

It is finished.

God is at rest, and invites us to rest with him in our souls.

We are free.

So let's let our imaginations and creative

energy run wild. Let's create a world we can be proud of. Let's let the pursuit of happiness and fulfillment be an equal opportunity for all people, everywhere.

Let's love each other with abandon.

Let's enjoy living in the Kingdom of God on earth.

Let's do this thing.

Bonus Essay:

What about The Great Commission?

Matthew 28:18-20 has had such importance in Evangelical theology it's been dubbed "The Great Commission."

But like any other piece of theology with a nickname (think: The Sermon on the Mount) it behooves us to make sure we're understanding it correctly.

Pastors and theologians have decided The Great Commission means to go into all the world and make disciples of Christ, baptizing them and teaching them to do all Jesus commanded.

That's exactly what the text says.

Sounds pretty simple, right? And we are doing our best to get it done.

But are we *understanding* it correctly?

I would argue we are not.

The Great Commission was meant to be this: Not a job or our mission, but *inviting* people to freedom and rest. The freedom and rest that Jesus *commanded* us to have (Matthew 11:28-30, Galatians 5:1).

Shortly after Jesus gave The Great Commission, he added an addendum that's been largely ignored when you hear someone speak on this subject: That the disciples were to *wait* until the Holy Spirit came (Acts 1:4) and *then*, in spiritual rest and freedom, they were simply to follow the Spirit's

143

lead.

If we continue to 'do' The Great Commission with the view of theology we have today, we will continue to make others twice the sons (and daughters) of hell we are. Not because we're hypocrites—as Jesus was charging certain Pharisees with that phrase—but because God never intended us to invite others into a life of *religion* or a *self-improvement plan to perfect ourselves* in self-effort (Galatians 3:3). He offers a life of rest and freedom, creativity, love and fulfillment.

With The Great Commission, Jesus was, as he always did, turning the Jewish way of life on its head. Disciples of Pharisaic Rabbis at that time were 'yoked' under the heavy burden of the Mosaic Law. Paul called this Law 'the ministry of death' (2 Corinthians 3:7).

So Jesus goes the opposite way.

To Jesus, making disciples meant inviting people to rest and freedom. That's what being a disciple of Christ meant *after* the cross.

Before the cross, he invited his disciples to see if they could live the Law perfectly with him; to out Pharisee the Pharisees, as it were (Matthew 5:20). They were set up to fail, in a way, and that's why Bible teachers for centuries always joke that the disciples, especially Peter, were such failures (but God loved them anyway, just like us....hahahha, blah, blah, blah).

The good news for us is that we are *not* to live the teachings of Jesus when he was teaching Law (Romans 7:6), therefore, we are *not* at risk of being seen by God, or by anyone else, as failures.

Imagine someone being called a failure at resting in freedom.

Is that possible?

Only if you live the opposite way, thinking there is still outstanding work to be done between you and God.

Only if you live religiously.

So let's choose to do the commands of Jesus that *weren't* the Law of Moses. Let's take him up on his offer to rest and simply live in freedom with the Spirit of God.

Appendix

Some long staid theological notions need to be questioned.

Not only questioned as in 'tweaked,' but as in, *are they really even biblical at all*? And if not, let's throw them out.

Here are a few notions that should probably go by the wayside:

1. The idea of 'sanctification.' That the goal of life is to become 'Christlike.'

There is strong anti-support of that idea in Galatians 2:20, where Paul says, in effect, I don't even exist when compared to Christ.

It's not that he is becoming *like* Christ, it's that he's fully letting Christ be Christ.

In this verse, Paul is not on a process of becoming more behaviorally like Jesus. Taken along with 'when I am weak, he is strong' we see that Paul is very comfortable being himself and having his own identity and responsibility for his existence, and Jesus clearly has a separate personality from Paul in the form of the Holy Spirit.

But here's the major problem with sanctification anyway: We 'try' to sanctify ourselves in our own effort and energy, which flies in the face of Galatians 3:3. Even though Christians say we are perfecting ourselves in the power of the Spirit, in reality, it's simply human power—it's behavior modification done by the pressure of ourselves and/or the church. It is rarely, if ever, done by God, because we have placed our energy above God's. We get in his way. This is why Jesus says to rest. This is why Paul says God shines through a jar of clay. This is why God is strong when we are weak. Jesus made us sanctified by the cross. We are *already* complete and lacking in nothing. Why would God then have us on a process of *becoming* sanctified?

It makes no sense.

Sure, I can become more mature when it comes to living a beneficial life instead of a harmful one. I can, over time, learn how to love people more effectively. But that doesn't mean my nature is being changed. My nature's already *been* changed. I *am* a new creation and it can't get any better than that. I have the full capacity right now to be incredibly loving, or not. It's not about character or nature change, it's about choice. Choosing to love. And love is an ungraspable and malleable thing. It's not something that can be measured in a 'growth' or 'process' sort of way.

So, yes, the notion of sanctification needs to go away. And sadly, nearly all of our theology is based on that.

So let's figure it out.

There *is* a better way.

2. Church in all its present forms needs to be thrown out.

Surprised?
I'm not.

This is the reason why everything in this book is hard to mention in 'church.' It's difficult to speak to an institution where the goal is for that institution to go away, and the faster the better.

This idea is not popular at all. Especially from those paid to run the place, because when we say church needs to go away, that includes all clergy, all paid professional Christians, and even career missionaries.

But I'm not including in that those who do ministries of social service. In other words, if someone is running a homeless shelter I wouldn't consider them to be a professional Christian, no matter what their beliefs. They are providing a social service, and in this way, the earth is being restored and renewed along the lines of Revelation 21 and 22. It furthers God's vision (the original vision of Genesis 1 and 2) for a restored creation whether intentional or not.

This is the 'good news' of the Bible: That creation is being healed and restored.

This *is* happening.

God *is* doing this.

And doing it through anyone who chooses to love.

3. We need to understand that church as we know it today is nothing like the gatherings of people in the New Testament 'churches.'

Our view of what church is comes from Roman Empire times when there was a state sanctioned 'church.' This is when most forms and trappings we know of today were put in place—liturgy, the recitation of creeds, paid clergy, etc.

It is said Paul was the first missionary and he planted 'churches.'

No, he did not.

Paul did not plant churches as we think of these gatherings today.

Paul supported the idea of groups of people who'd opted for freedom to meet together because he knew they needed a safe environment to support each other since they lived in extremely difficult times. The days were indeed evil.

As mentioned in the above story, Paul's 'church' gatherings were comprised of those who were dropping out of the two major shackling systems of the day—following the 613 Laws of Moses, and pagan ritual evil.

In our day, neither of those oppressive systems exist, so we don't need pockets of humans supporting each other to counter those endeavors. We, especially in the United States, have a wide berth of freedom and creativity in organizing ourselves to participate in God's healing and restoring of creation in an infinite number of ways. We are lucky in that our social systems largely reflect our freedom before God. We live in freedom with respect to religion, socially and politically. We do not have two shackling systems causing persecution unto death hanging over our heads.

We simply don't.

So how, when, and why we gather needs to be completely rethought.

Which leads to the next point...

4. What should replace 'church' as we know it

today? We know it's outdated and outmoded. So what to do?

Well, I believe we should still meet together in groups of loving communities of people.

Nothing wrong with that.

But what is the goal when we meet?

We now know 'worship' was never meant to be the main goal for believers meeting together. We also know we no longer need just one so-called expert to interpret the Bible for us.

So what to do?

That is where freedom comes in. And where things get exciting.

We have total freedom to be as creative as possible when we meet together. It can be as simple as enjoying each other's company.

Simply watching movies perhaps.

Maybe we'll have parties and enjoy community in all the infinite ways it can be enjoyed.

If we choose, we can get together to discuss ways to participate in the renewing, restoring and caring for the health of all of creation, individually and corporately. As Paul says a billion times and emphasizes in 1 Corinthians 13—we can talk about how to love. And we can love while we rest and piggy-back on God's energy, just as it was done in the book of Acts. We can hang out until the Holy Spirit guides us.

But, you might say, who's to say how or by what means the Holy Spirit is guiding? Doesn't someone need to lead? What happens if everyone has their own individual idea of where the Holy Spirit is leading?

What then?

Well, there's nothing wrong if some do one

thing, and others do something else for a time. Or maybe everyone will support each other as they do individual projects. It doesn't matter. We have infinite freedom and the widest berth possible for creativity. Let's make use of it. The only criteria for whether the Holy Spirit is involved in something, or not, is this—Is it loving, or not? And this can be discussed as a group, and *should* be discussed as a group.

Is it *really* that hard to tell if something is done in love or not? True, the road to Hell can be paved with good intentions—but that is the great thing about *community*—more voices enable us to get things right. And if it's not right, we can simply stop doing that and make any amends that need to be made and change course.

But wouldn't that mean what we thought was the guidance of the Holy Spirit wasn't the Holy Spirit at all? After all, would God make mistakes?

Well, short of having God speak to us directly collectively, I think in time, as humanity is more and more restored, what is loving and what isn't will become clearer and clearer. God is still involved, and this is where the Bible, of course, is still tremendously valuable. The Bible is the autobiography of the definition of love itself: God. We can, and should, make utmost use of it. There is a lot of love happening in the Bible that we can look to for guidance and examples.

And that leads to the next thing that needs to be rethought and thrown out:

5. Portrayals of God that are negative and unloving.

Who needs a crap-God you wouldn't even want for a parent? It seems strange that we ascribe attitudes and actions to God that are incredibly unloving and negative. It's even more odd that theologians seem to have an aversion to portraying God in a positive light. Sometimes he's sacrificial and really cool, then he turns around and seemingly makes people suffer, or does something equally as negative, in order to get his 'will' done or to teach us a lesson.

Strange.

For instance, John 5:1-15. I've always heard this healing event is about Jesus confronting a guy about his bad attitude. Supposedly, as the sermon traditionally goes, the man remained unhealed by the pool for years because he was comfortable in his impaired state and consciously didn't want to be healed because then he'd have to take responsibility for his life.

Interesting how well this fits American politically conservative notions about welfare and laziness and not being willing to work or take care of oneself. But I hardly think this is what John had in mind.

This is *not* an American story about working, or being comfortable not working. *Obviously* not. It is a story of God breaking into the natural world to supernaturally heal a man's life *regardless* of his attitude. Jesus comes on the scene with an invitation from God: *Do you want to be healed?*

Jesus doesn't ask this with a sarcastic emphasis on 'want,' as if questioning the man's motives.

No.

He's asking because the guy has been there a

long time and now the true healer has not only broken into human history, but is standing right there in his midst.

And Jesus is *excited* to heal him.

"*Do you want to be healed?*" he asks with excitement, knowing the man's whole life is about to change.

And it's fantastic.

It's a fantastic scene.

So we see that God is *not* being a sarcastic jerk. So let's not portray him that way.

* * *

Ok, this list could stretch on into infinity, but that's enough to get us started.

Let's continue to talk.

Let's keep this thing rolling.

Let's present a better view of God and the Bible to ourselves, and to the rest of the world.

Thanks for listening.

Acknowledgments

Though one name appears on the cover of a book, it's quite true that a book can hardly be produced by one person.

It's always a team effort.

It has to be.

The project is so enormous there's no way one person can carry it alone. That's why there are more people to thank than I could possibly fit on these pages. Truly everyone I've ever known has had a hand in the making of this book.

It's difficult to name people without the painful reality that some who deserve mention will be left out. So I'll try to stick with a short list in order not to fill five more books of print.

As usual, Pamela Sibert Hooker has done more work than anyone on the planet in helping me produce these books. She is amazing at layout and all things technical, as well as an excellent editor. Not only that, she's a great friend. The best sort of friend anyone could ever ask for.

Another extraordinary editor, Melanie Harvey, poured in so much work on past projects she deserves a special mention here as well. 'Thank You' is simply not powerful enough to express my appreciation for all you've done, Melanie. Words will always fail.

My siblings Steve and Brian have been with me every step of the way on this massive theological revamping of everything. The ideas contained herein are as much theirs as they are mine. We've had countless hours of discussion amongst ourselves and with others, and it's my hope that this will continue long into the future.

To everyone I've ever known and to those I see everyday—

Thank you.

This project belongs to all of us.

About the Author

D. Harold is a journalist and author that has been involved in churches and small group Bible studies for more than 35 years. Originally from the central Ohio area, he divides his time between Florida, Colorado and the Middle East.

www.ingramcontent.com/pod-product-compliance
Lightning Source LLC
Chambersburg PA
CBHW031959040426

42448CB00006B/427